Feb. 25

W9-BBE-317

AN INTIMATE JOURNAL OF
THE DREYFUS CASE

AN
INTIMATE JOURNAL
OF
The Dreyfus Case

MAURICE PALÉOLOGUE

CRITERION BOOKS   NEW YORK

Copyright © 1957 by Criterion Books, Inc.
Library of Congress catalog card no. 56-11400

Translated from the French by Eric Mosbacher

Manufactured in the United States of America
American Book–Stratford Press, Inc., New York

FOREWORD

On November 1, 1886, Maurice Paléologue, then aged twenty-seven and for the past four years an embassy secretary, was assigned to the "reserved affairs" section of the political department of the French Ministry of Foreign Affairs. This was the name discreetly given to what was, in fact, a kind of intelligence service belonging to the Quai d'Orsay in its own right; certain police investigations ended up in the "reserved affairs" section, which was also responsible for certain confidential contacts with the Ministry of War. Thus by the very nature of his employment, Maurice Paléologue was for many years brought into constant and regular contact with the army intelligence service. He was frequently called on to work in close collaboration with officers engaged in espionage or counterespionage work. Moreover, as a reserve artillery lieutenant from 1891 onward, he was assigned to the offices of the intelligence service in the Ministry of War during his annual training period.

He, therefore, came naturally to be involved in the inner developments of the Dreyfus case. As early as October 16, 1894, that is to say, barely three weeks after the discovery of the famous *bordereau* [1] among papers abstracted from the German Embassy, Colonel Sandherr, the chief of the army intelligence service, asked him for copies of all messages and telegrams from foreign embassies and chancelleries in Paris intercepted by the Quai d'Orsay which might throw light on his inquiries. A few days later Gabriel Hanotaux, the Minister of Foreign Affairs, gave him official instructions to follow the case on behalf of his department; and these instructions were confirmed by Delcassé, Hanotaux's successor. In 1899 Paléologue had the task of submitting the "diplomatic file" on the case to the Cour de Cassation and to the second Rennes court-martial. Five years earlier, in the uniform of an artillery officer and standing at Colonel Sandherr's side, he had been present at the ceremonial degradation of Captain Dreyfus on the esplanade of the Champ-de-Mars. Hence the interest of the diary kept daily by the young diplomatist during the course of these tragically agitated years.

In 1942 the author submitted the manuscript of this book to the Librairie Plon in Paris, under the title, "French Diplomacy and the Dreyfus Case," with

[1] *I.e.,* "list." It will be referred to throughout in the French form by which it is universally known.

authority to publish it four years after his death. Historical objectivity makes it necessary to admit that the text does not correspond exactly with that of the diary of the years 1894–99. Maurice Paléologue recast and pruned his daily notes. He arranged them into a tale of powerful dramatic interest, a tragedy in five acts, which also possesses the excitement of a detective novel, in which the truth comes to light only slowly and gradually. Maurice Paléologue made no attempt to deny the literary retouching to which he subjected his diary; he insisted, however, that the process in no way affected the genuineness of the document. "As for my Dreyfus case diary," he wrote to the literary director of the Librairie Plon in May, 1942, "there is in existence no copy, typewritten version, or papers of any kind other than the document that I have delivered to you. If I destroyed the manuscript of my diary, it is because I wrote it each evening, and it consequently contained many details that have become insignificant; I also noted down many intimate conversations that I have no right to use. Finally, to attest the accuracy and genuineness of the said diary, the text of my official telegrams, of which there are copies at the Quai d'Orsay, gives you every guarantee."

The reader will easily convince himself of the historical importance to be attached to the publication of this diary. Some will probably criticize the author for a rather too obvious pleasure in the picturesque anecdote, the romantic explanation, the pathos of gesture and attitude. Others will regret the severity of certain personal judgments, which perhaps should be accepted with reserve. Maurice Paléologue was too closely involved in the controversies let loose by the Dreyfus case for his detachment to be complete. He lived in close contact with the chief figures of the drama. He received the confidences of Colonel Sandherr, Major Henry, General Gonse, and General de Boisdeffre. He was involved in the daily tasks of the information service and was aware of most of its intrigues. He discovered or "smelled out" many secrets never mentioned in official documents or court records. He circulated freely behind the scenes in certain military, diplomatic, and parliamentary quarters that few have ever penetrated. Certain psychological aspects of the origin of the Dreyfus case become intelligible only after reading Paléologue's story.

Also Maurice Paléologue puts forward an entirely new version of the espionage affair that led to Captain Dreyfus' conviction in 1894. According to what he says under the date January 3, 1899, "the act of treason that supplied the motive for securing Dreyfus' conviction" should be "associated with a chain of similar events that began in 1886 and continued to 1896." Dreyfus having been cleared of all suspicion, there was not one traitor, but three: that strange adventurer Esterhazy; a familiar of the supreme commander, General Saussier, named Maurice Weil; and finally an "officer of very high rank," "on whom no suspicion yet rests," "who, after holding important office for several years at the Ministry of War, is now in command of troops." Who is this third man, this mysterious "X" of high military rank? The author's reticence can only be regretted. There is no doubt, however, that he provides an unexpected trail which many investigators will now follow.

The text of the diary submitted to the Librairie Plon is translated in full in this volume, together with some supplementary notes by the author. A number of biographical notes have been added to make it easier for the contemporary reader to follow the essential episodes and principal characters. It is for historians of the Third Republic to decide whether the former diplomatist's diary puts a final full-stop to the massive literature on the subject, or adds new points of interrogation.

CONTENTS

1. RIDDLE OF 1894

1. RIDDLE OF 1894

Friday, October 12, 1894

Nisard,[1] the director of political affairs, sent for me this morning, and said to me, in a rather strange manner:

"Have you been to the information department these last few days?"

"No."

"Has no officer been to see you?"

"No."

---

[1] Armand Nisard, born 1841, was in 1889 chief French delegate on the commission charged with the preparatory work for the delimitation of British and French possessions on the west coast of Africa, and at the end of that year became director of political affairs and head of the legal department at the Quai d'Orsay. He retained this position until 1898, when he was appointed French Ambassador to the Holy See. He retired in 1904 and died twenty years later.

Then, under the seal of secrecy, he told me the following:

A conference of Ministers took place yesterday at the Place Beauvau. There were present: Charles Dupuy, the Prime Minister;[2] General Mercier, the Minister of War; Guérin, the Keeper of the Seals; and Hanotaux, the Minister of Foreign Affairs.

General Mercier,[3] who caused this meeting to be held, said that a counter-espionage agent had recently abstracted from the German Embassy a letter the anonymous author of which informed Major von Schwartzkoppen, the military attaché, that he had sent him five more or less secret documents. The nature of the latter makes it plain beyond dispute that the traitor is on the General Staff. Other indications, and in particular a striking similarity of handwriting, point clearly to his identity. In view of the gravity of the matter, General Mercier, before informing the Council of Ministers, thought it advisable to consult the three

[2] The formation by Charles Dupuy (1851–1923) of a Cabinet of young men, including Poincaré, Hanotaux, and Delcassé, in May, 1893, marked the change in ministerial personnel that followed the Panama scandal. Dupuy was again summoned to power in May, 1894, by Sadi Carnot, and retained office until January, 1895. He was Prime Minister for a third time from November, 1898, to June, 1899.

[3] Auguste Mercier (1833–1921) took part in the Mexican campaign and fought in the war of 1870. In 1888 he became director of administrative services in the War Ministry and was given command of the 18th Corps in 1893. He served as War Minister in the Casimir-Perier Cabinet (1893–94) and in the second Dupuy Cabinet (1894–95). He was elected Nationalist senator for the Loire-Inférieure in 1900.

of his colleagues most directly concerned. He did not mention the suspected officer's name.

Charles Dupuy and Guérin, who were very upset, examined the various possible courses of action that might be taken without being able to make up their minds. Only Hanotaux [4] categorically declared: "If you have no evidence other than this letter and a similarity of handwriting, I am opposed to any judicial proceedings and even to any investigation. The national interest is at stake." By this firm language, he obtained from Mercier an assurance that no proceedings would be taken unless further evidence was obtained.

During the evening Hanotaux went to see Mercier in the Rue St. Dominique and again did his utmost to convince him that, the letter having been stolen from the German Embassy, its production before a court-martial, even *in camera,* would involve the risk of provoking the gravest international difficulties. "As it is

[4] Gabriel Hanotaux, born 1853, started his career as archivist at the Quai d'Orsay and served as principal private secretary to the Minister of Foreign Affairs in the governments of Gambetta (1881) and Jules Ferry (1883–85). After a brief period in the French Embassy in Constantinople, he was elected Republican deputy for the Aisne. In 1889, when he failed to be re-elected, he returned to the service of the Foreign Ministry, where he was appointed to the grade of minister-plenipotentiary and served in turn as deputy director of protectorates and director of commercial affairs. In May, 1894, Charles Dupuy entrusted him with the portfolio of Foreign Affairs, which he retained in the Ribot Cabinet until November, 1895, and reassumed in the Méline Cabinet (May, 1896–June, 1898) He retired from politics in 1898, after the Fashoda crisis, to devote himself exclusively to his career as a historian. He died in 1944.

the decisive piece of evidence, and as in consequence
the whole trial would hinge on it, you would be unable
to prevent the newspapers from publishing it, no matter what you did. Just imagine the uproar that that
would lead to!'' The general replied that the law com-
pelled him to pursue such a patent and well-established
crime. Moreover, he pointed out that, as a number of
officers and several experts were already aware of the
matter, failure to bring the traitor to justice would inevitably leak out, thus leading to a scandal of a different kind. ''I do not wish to be accused of having com-
pounded with treason.'' So the law is to take its course.
Hanotaux left in a rage.

When Nisard had come to the end of his confidences,
he asked me if I knew how the intelligence service procured papers from the German Embassy. General
Mercier had said that the letter had reached the General Staff by ''the ordinary route.'' What was this
''ordinary route''? Hanotaux attached great importance to being informed on this point.

I explained to him how the ''ordinary route''
worked.

''The intelligence service,'' I said, ''has succeeded
in suborning a servant at the German Embassy. She is
a woman of about forty. She is named Marie Bastian,
vulgar, stupid, and completely illiterate, but she has,
nevertheless, been clever enough to gain the confidence
of her employers. She is the charwoman; she washes
down the stairs, cleans the windows, lights the fires,
and sweeps out the offices, and she has the run of the
house all day long. It is thus very easy for her to pick

up papers that embassy secretaries or military attachés
tear up and put in the wastepaper basket. She periodi-
cally hands them over to another counter-espionage
agent, Brücker, or sometimes to an officer of the intelligence service. The hand-over generally takes place in
the evening, in a chapel of St. Clotilda.''

''But how is it possible for anyone to be so foolish
as to put papers of any value in the wastepaper basket,
even after tearing them up?'' Nisard exclaimed, raising his arms. ''How is it that they are not burned?''

''How are you to deal with negligence? Do you sup-
pose that in our offices . . . ?''

''Don't go on!''

''To conclude with the 'ordinary route,' I have no
need to tell you that I know neither the agent Brücker
nor the woman Bastian. I know they exist and how they
work, and that is enough for me.'' [5]

Tuesday, October 16, 1894

Colonel Sandherr [6] has just brought me his periodical

[5] Mme Bastian at first handed over the papers to the agent
Brücker. The latter, however, having become suspect at the end of
1893, she entered into direct contact with officers of the intelligence
service: first Captain Rollin and subsequently Major Henry. Major
Henry sorted the torn documents and fitted together those written
in French; those written in German he passed on to Captain Lauth.
After the fragments had been sorted and fitted together, they were
submitted to the chief of the service. Mme Bastian continued with
her espionage work until July 15, 1899. Then, fearing that she
might be ordered to appear at the Rennes court-martial, she stopped
working for the German Embassy and retired to live at Marly. The
War Ministry ceased all payments to her in November, 1899.

[6] Jean Sandherr was born at Mulhouse in 1846. He graduated from

bulletin of secret documents and information. Contrary
to his habit, he did not stop to talk; he did not even
sit down.

"I've only dropped in for a moment," he said. "I'm
very busy today."

Just when he was leaving, he fixed his policeman's
eyes on me—eyes as penetrating as they are impenetrable—and said in a grave voice:

"We're engaged in a very delicate business . . . a bad
business, and Schwartzkoppen's in it again, caught
red-handed.[7] So if you find out anything whatever

St. Cyr in 1866 and was a regimental officer until 1885, when he
went to the École de Guerre. In 1891 he was appointed chief of the
"statistical section"—or intelligence department—of the War Ministry, with the rank of lieutenant-colonel. In 1894, serving under
Colonel Sandherr, in this section were: Major Cordier, Major Henry,
Captain Matton, Captain Lauth, and Gribelin, the administrative
officer and archivist. On July 1, 1895, Lieutenant-Colonel Picquart
was appointed by General de Boisdeffre to succeed Sandherr as
chief of the intelligence service, and the latter assumed command
of the 20th Battalion of Infantry at Montauban. He died in 1897.

[7] Lieutenant-Colonel Max von Schwartzkoppen was military attaché in the German Embassy in Paris. He was born at Potsdam in
1850, the son of a general who was Military Governor of Berlin, and
served as an infantry lieutenant in the campaign of 1870–71. He became a captain on the General Staff in 1882 and was sent to Paris,
where he remained until 1885, as second military attaché. He was
then sent to Darmstadt as military instructor to the heir of the
Grand Duke of Hesse. After various military commands, he returned
to Paris as first military attaché in the autumn of 1891. He became
lieutenant-colonel in 1893, aide-de-camp to the Kaiser in 1896,
colonel in 1897. He ceased to be military attaché in Paris in November, 1897. Schwartzkoppen directed espionage operations in co-
operation with the Italian military attaché, Panizzardi; he was, in
consequence, a frequent object of attack in the French press.

about what he has been up to, particularly if your decoders pick up any snatch of his telegraphic correspondence, don't fail to let me know.''

"I think I can guess what case you're alluding to."

"Oh? What do you know?"

"I know everything that your Minister said to mine,
but that's all. So I don't know the name of the in-
criminated officer."

"You soon will. Besides, I shall soon be coming to
tell you all about it because I think you will be able to
help us a great deal. . . . It's a shocking case!''

"Are the facts certain?"

"As certain as I'm standing here. . . . The evidence
is overwhelming!"

Friday, October 26, 1894

A visit from Colonel Sandherr.

He told me under the seal of secrecy that the incrim-
inated officer is a Jew, Captain Alfred Dreyfus, who
has just concluded a long period in the various bureaus
of the General Staff. He was thus well able to document
himself. Besides, his indiscreet curiosity, his continual
ferreting about, his mysterious ways, and finally his
sly and vain character, "betraying all the pride and
all the ignominy of his race," had rendered him suspect for a long time. He was put in the Cherche-Midi
prison on the fifteenth of this month. The inquiries in
progress leave no doubt about his guilt.[8]

[8] The state of the inquiries on October 26, 1894, could be summed
up as follows: the letter or list, the famous *bordereau,* which had
been received by Major Henry with other papers from the German
Embassy between September 24 and September 26, had by General

To make his investigations as conclusive as possible, Sandherr asked me to search our secret information for the years 1893 and 1894 for anything that might

---

Mercier's orders been submitted to the chiefs of the four bureaus of the General Staff and then photographed; proofs of the photograph had been passed round the various departments of the Ministry, and examination of them had yielded no result. But the general opinion was that the author of the *bordereau* must be an artilleryman and belong to the General Staff. On October 5 Colonel Fabre, chief of the Fourth Bureau, had shown the document to his deputy, Lieutenant-Colonel d'Aboville, when he returned from leave. Both formed the opinion that it must be the work of an officer who had been assigned for instruction to all four bureaus of the General Staff. They looked up the files of those who had been attached to the General Staff for instruction and noticed a resemblance between the writing of the *bordereau* and that of Captain Dreyfus. On October 6 General Mercier instructed Major du Paty de Clam to carry out a more thorough investigation. On October 7 Major du Paty submitted his conclusions to General Gonse, the Deputy Chief of the General Staff: "In short, in spite of certain differences, there is sufficient resemblance between the two handwritings to justify an expert appraisal." On October 13 the expert Gobert, nominated by Guérin, the Keeper of the Seals, submitted his report, the conclusion of which was that the *bordereau* "might have emanated from an individual other than that suspected." General Gonse, desiring another opinion, submitted the documents to Alphonse Bertillon, chief of the photographic department at the Préfecture of Police, who decided that the writers were identical. Dreyfus was ordered to attend an inspection of officers attached for instruction to the General Staff at 9 A.M. on October 15. He duly presented himself at the office of General de Boisdeffre, the Chief of the General Staff, where he was arrested by Major du Paty de Clam. He vigorously protested his innocence. Du Paty showed him a revolver that had been concealed under a file and encouraged him to "do the right thing." Dreyfus refused and continued to maintain his innocence. He was immediately taken to the Cherche-Midi prison.

On the same day a search was carried out at the home of Mme Dreyfus and on the next day at that of M. Hadamard, Dreyfus'

appear to be related to the crime of which Captain
Dreyfus is accused. He ended with these words:

"Tomorrow I shall send you Major Henry, who, as
you know, is our counter-espionage specialist. He will
be of great help to you in your search."

I reported Sandherr's call to Nisard who, after con-
ferring with the Minister, gave me authority to hand
over any document that might seem to me to be help-
ful to the cause of military justice.

Saturday, October 27, 1894

I found no document or piece of information in our
secret information files having even the remotest connection with the treasonable activity attributed to Captain Dreyfus.

All the same, to satisfy my conscience, I showed
Major Henry my files. He gleaned no more than I did.

After this fruitless search, we talked. Thus I learned
how the letter reached the General Staff. As I assumed,
it was among a lot of papers abstracted by Marie

---

father-in-law, but without result. On October 18, 20, 22, and 24, Du
Paty interrogated Dreyfus and made him write out various texts.
This yielded no results, and Dreyfus continued his protestations of
innocence. The whole of Major du Paty's interrogation, which continued until October 30, was directed toward obtaining a confession
from him that he was the author of the *bordereau,* which remained
the only evidence supporting the charge. Meanwhile, as the expert
opinions of Gobert and Bertillon canceled each other out, three
other experts were called in—Charavay, Pelletier, and Teyssonnières.
On October 26 only Pelletier's report, which was favorable to Dreyfus, had been received. The other two, which were unfavorable, were
not received until October 29.

Bastian, who on this occasion handed over her booty to Henry direct.[9]

Thursday, November 1, 1894

The *Figaro* publishes the following, under the heading "A case of treason":

Grave presumptive evidence has led to the provisional arrest of a French officer suspected of having communicated to foreigners some documents of little importance. The truth must be made known very quickly.

But the *Libre Parole*,[10] the newspaper of Drumont,

[9] The text of the *bordereau* abstracted from the German Embassy of which Captain Dreyfus was accused of being the author was as follows:

Though without news indicating that you desire to see me, nevertheless, sir, I send you some interesting information.
(1) A note on the hydraulic buffer of the 120 and the way in which this gun behaves.
(2) A note on the covering troops (some modifications will be introduced under the new plan).
(3) A note on a modification to the artillery formations.
(4) A note about Madagascar.
(5) The draft field artillery firing manual (March 14, 1894).
This last document is very difficult to obtain, and I can have it at my disposal for only a very few days. The War Ministry has sent a fixed number to the corps, and the corps are responsible for them; each officer who has a copy must return it after the maneuvers. If, therefore, you wish to extract what interests you and hold it at my disposal afterward, I shall fetch it. Unless you would like me to have it copied *in extenso* and send you a copy.
I am just off on maneuvers.
[10] The *Libre Parole* was founded in 1892, six years after the publication of *la France juive* had gained its author immense celebrity. Edouard Drumont was a deputy for Paris from 1898 to 1902. In 1899 he published *les Juifs et l'affaire Dreyfus*.

the standard-bearer of anti-Semitism, has not hesitated to make a complete disclosure. It prints in huge letters: "High Treason! Arrest of a Jewish officer, Captain Dreyfus."

Poincaré, surprised and even indignant at these disclosures which he had been given no reason to foresee, telephoned to Charles Dupuy and asked him to call an urgent Cabinet meeting.

Though it was All Saints' Day, the Ministers met immediately at the Place Beauvau.

The meeting began with an exchange of bitter-sweet observations; Poincaré, Delcassé, Leygues, and Barthou [11] did not conceal their dissatisfaction at not having been informed earlier. General Mercier then gave his colleagues an account of the results of his investigations. Hanotaux persisted in his objections to a prosecution. After this the Cabinet unanimously resolved to open a judicial inquiry into Captain Dreyfus.

Friday, November 2, 1894

The Emperor Alexander III died yesterday at Livadia.

The President of the Republic had asked to see the principal documents about the Franco-Russian alliance, particularly those which foresee military cooperation. I was instructed to take them to him, as they are in my charge, and this provided the occasion for a long and intimate conversation with him. [12]

[11] Poincaré was Finance Minister, Delcassé Minister for the Colonies, Leygues Education Minister, and Barthou Minister of Public Works.

[12] *Author's note:* In the following pages I frequently mention my

The conversation left me with a great feeling of sadness. For various reasons, not all of them of a political nature, Casimir-Perier has taken such a dislike to his Presidential functions that he no longer thinks of anything but resigning. In spite of all that I was able to say to him, which added but a feeble note to the remonstrances of his mother, his wife, and his brother-in-law, Louis de Ségur, he kept using such expressions as "the prison of the Élysée," "It is very charitable of you to come and see me in my prison," "Ah! When shall I escape from this galley?"

Everything was an excuse to unbosom himself to me. Thus, talking about yesterday's unexpected meeting of Ministers to discuss the Dreyfus case, which, like all Cabinet meetings, was held without him, he said: "My Ministers do without me. Very well! But one of these days I'll do without them—and their successors!" It is becoming a fixed idea, a compulsive obsession, an anxiety neurosis.[13]

---

close relations with the President of the Republic. Such intimacy between the chief of state and a mere embassy secretary might be surprising to those unaware that I had for a long time been honored with M. Casimir-Perier's friendship, to such an extent that he had made me his principal private secretary when he was appointed Prime Minister and Foreign Minister in 1893.

[13] Jean Casimir-Perier (1847–1907) was Prime Minister from April to December, 1893. He became President of the Republic in June, 1894, after the assassination of Sadi Carnot. Having proclaimed his intention of making full use of the rights conferred upon him by the constitution, he was subjected to daily attacks from the Left, which denounced him as the principal shareholder of the Anzin mines. He resigned on January 15, 1895, embittered by the election as a deputy for Paris of the journalist Gérault-Richard,

Saturday, November 3, 1894

General Saussier,[14] the military governor of Paris, ordered proceedings to be taken in connection with the crime of treason imputed to Captain Dreyfus.

The case has been entrusted to Major d'Ormescheville, judge-advocate to the Army Council.

Monday, November 5, 1894

Our cryptographers, who have acquired fantastic skill in the enthralling and cabalistic art of decoding or, as it used to be called, "scrutinizing" the coded correspondence of foreign embassies, have for the past three days been exerting themselves to unravel a logogriph which will perhaps provide us with the whole secret of the Dreyfus case.

It is a telegram sent on November 2 by Lieutenant-Colonel Panizzardi, the Italian military attaché, to

---

who was serving a term of imprisonment for outrages against the chief of state, and disappointed at his inability to exercise any real control or influence over the Government.

[14] Felix Saussier (1828–1905) had seen active service in Africa, the Crimea, Italy, and Mexico. In the war of 1870 he was colonel of a regiment of the line and took part in the fighting near Metz. He was taken prisoner and sent to Germany but escaped and rejoined the Army of the Loire, in which he was given command of a brigade. In 1873 he was elected to the National Assembly and sat with the Left-Center. In 1879 he was in comand of the 19th Corps, and in 1881 the Government gave him the command of the Tunisian expedition. He was appointed Military Governor of Paris in 1884 and subsequently vice-president of the Army Council, that is to say commander-in-chief designate in the event of war; he remained until 1898 the principal military personality in the country.

General Marselli, the Chief of the General Staff in Rome.

The task to which our decoders, our "hierophants," as Nisard calls them, are applying themselves is particularly difficult because the cipher used by Lieutenant-Colonel Panizzardi is new and entirely unknown. It is thus not just a matter of unraveling a coded text; first, the key to the whole cipher, that is to say, the law of the esoteric system, has to be discovered, its vocabulary, with its combinations of "cadence" and "variation." This divinatory labor necessarily implies a large number of calculations, hypotheses, drafts, and approximations.

Nevertheless the meaning of the telegram is already emerging; one would almost be justified in concluding that Panizzardi had not been in contact with Dreyfus.

Colonel Sandherr, whom I at once informed, immediately sent one of his officers to see me, Captain Matton, who showed the liveliest interest in our discovery, in spite of the doubts and reservations to which it is still subject.

Tuesday, November 6, 1894

The elucidation of the Panizzardi telegram is advancing rapidly; only the last three words are still in doubt. The translation reads: "If Captain Dreyfus has not had dealings with you, it would be advisable to instruct the Embassy to publish an official denial. (Our emissary warned?)"

The cipher service has unofficially submitted this

version to Colonel Sandherr, drawing his attention to the conjectural nature of the last three words.

Wednesday, November 7, 1894

General de Boisdeffre, the Chief of the General Staff,[15] has been appointed special ambassador to attend the funeral of the Emperor Alexander III.

The distinguished role that he played in 1892 as negotiator of the military convention[16] qualifies him better than anyone else for this exalted mission.

I have been given the task of drafting the instructions with which he will be provided in view of the conversations that he will be having with the new Czar.

Saturday, November 10, 1894

The Panizzardi telegram has been completely deci-

[15] Charles de Boisdeffre (1839–1919) had been military attaché in St. Petersburg, 1879–80. He became Deputy Chief of the General Staff in 1890, and Chief of the General Staff in 1893. He carried out several missions to Russia, in 1892 as negotiator of the military convention, in 1894 as leader of the French mission that attended the funeral of Alexander III, and in 1896 at the coronation of Nicholas II. He resigned his post as Chief of the General Staff after the discovery of the Henry forgery.

[16] The military convention of July, 1892, was the key document in the Franco-Russian alliance to which the political agreement of August 5, 1891, was preliminary. The 1892 convention, the duration of which was limited only by that of the Triple Alliance (Germany, Austria, and Italy) and remained secret, foresaw the immediate intervention of the forces of the other contracting party in the event of German aggression against either. It was ratified in December, 1893, and January, 1894, by an exchange of letters between Sadi Carnot and Alexander III.

phered. This is its exact meaning: "If Captain Dreyfus has not had dealings with you, it would be advisable
to instruct the Ambassador to publish an official denial
to avoid comments in the press."

If it is noted that this telegram was sent on November 2, that is to say, the day after Dreyfus' arrest became known, it becomes obvious that the Italian military attaché had no relations with him. Only the
German military attaché remains implicated.

As there was no longer any doubt about the purport
of the telegram, an official copy was sent immediately
to the Ministry of War.

I made a point of verifying all the deciphering work
for myself, and I believe myself entitled to say that it
reflects the greatest credit on the ingenuity of our
"hierophants." Every word of the text they have just
established is based on a synthesis of irrefutable facts.

Let me add an anecdotic detail. The cipher used by
the Italian officer to compose his cryptogram is a dic-
tionary to be found in commerce, the *Cifrario di Bara-
velli,* which he perfected for his own use by a skillful
transposition of all the numerical indices. Now, the
copy of the *Cifrario* on which our decoders worked has
its history: *Habent sua fata libelli!*

The intelligence service informed us in June last of
a mysterious correspondence carried on daily in coded
telegrams between the Count of Turin, a nephew of
King Umberto of Italy, and the Duchessa Grazioli, an
Italian living at the Hotel Windsor in Paris.

Colonel Sandherr, like a true *gendarme,* said to me:

"These telegrams don't smell good to me; to me there's a whiff of espionage about them."

I answered:

"This time, my dear colonel, your flair is deceiving you. To me these coded telegrams seem to give off a delicious perfume, for I know the lady who sends or receives them, the beautiful Duchessa Grazioli, Donna Nicoletta. She is a superb creature, tall, supple, and as voluptuous as a bacchante. All her days and all her nights are not long enough for the caprices of her private life, and I assure you that she has something better to do with her time than to engage in espionage."

But my romantic explanation failed to convince Sandherr, a skeptic by profession.

Not long afterward—it was on a Monday—he burst into my office, with a gleam of exhilaration in his eyes.

"Look!" he said, handing me a small, flat book bound in blue cloth. "Look! There's your duchessa's cipher! I've brought it so that your decoders can have a look at her correspondence with the Count of Turin."

"How did you get hold of it?"

"Oh, that was easy! The Duchessa Grazioli lives at the Hotel Windsor. I had her watched by one of my agents. Well, yesterday, Sunday, she went to the races. My man took advantage of the opportunity to slip into her room and search her trunks, her wardrobes, her bed, her clothes. . . ."

"And the hotel servants let him?"

"The hotel servants? Naturally I had given them something to keep their eyes shut."

"Naturally, that was the indispensable preliminary, I should have realized. . . . And the cipher?"

"In the end my agent found it in a very pretty toilet necessity, underneath a packet of fine handkerchiefs. Also it has a delicious scent. Smell it!"

"You're quite right, the scent is delicious. . . . You see how right I was the other day when I told you that your flair had deceived you!"

"Yes. . . . All that's left now is to see what is in the telegrams."

"Your curiosity shall soon be satisfied."

Two days later I took Sandherr the translation of his mysterious telegrams. Indeed they contained no suspicion of espionage. The decoded correspondence was perfectly clear and frank, for it expressed nothing but simple, elemental, natural feelings.

However, one four-figure sequence which recurred in most of the telegrams remained indecipherable. All that our decoders were able to suggest was that the apocalyptic number stood for something extraordinary, unforgettable, and sublime.

Perhaps it is this slim blue volume, this immodest *Cifrario,* which will show us whether Dreyfus is innocent or guilty.

Monday, November 12, 1894

The mission that is to represent France at the funeral of the Emperor Alexander III leaves for St. Petersburg tomorrow, so today I took to General de Boisdeffre Hanotaux's final instructions, as well as some information that reached us from Russia this morning.

After taking note of both, the Chief of the General Staff reminded me in friendly fashion of the now distant occasion of our first meeting.

This was in March, 1881, at the funeral of another Czar, the noble and chivalrous Alexander II, who was the emancipator of the *muzhiks* and the liberator of the Bulgarians, and who was assassinated by the Nihilists. Our Ambassador at that time was General Chanzy. Two of my friends, Ternaux-Compans and Melchior de Vogüé, were among his secretaries, and Lieutenant-Colonel de Boisdeffre was the military attaché. As for myself, then a novice in the profession of diplomacy, it was only by chance that I happened to be in St. Petersburg, as a courier.

Boisdeffre, with his usual graciousness, took pleasure in reviving our common memories. He summoned up in succession before my eyes the commanding presence of General Chanzy; the tragic spectacle of the Russian capital, a prey to the growing audacity of the Terrorists; the Byzantine pomp of the funeral ceremonies, the glittering and mysterious liturgy for the dead in the fortress church; and, the final act, the sudden appearance of the morganatic wife, Princess Yurievski, who came and burst into tears over the open coffin. He concluded:

"What I shall see this time will certainly be less theatrical. But how much graver the hour is for us now! Consider that the whole future of the alliance is at stake, and hence the whole strength and security of our country. What are the true feelings of the new Czar? What are the influences to which he will be sub-

jected? What hopes, what certainties, can we build on
him? .... As soon as I return, come and see me, my
dear Paléologue; I shall tell you my impressions.''

At the door, he whispered into my ear:

''What is happening between your Minister and M.
Casimir-Perier? What have they against each other?''

''I don't really know. .... I like to think that it is
merely a misunderstanding that will soon be cleared
up.''

After leaving Boisdeffre, I had myself announced
to the Deputy Chief of the General Staff, General
Gonse, under whom the intelligence service came.[17] I
found Colonel Sandherr in his office, finishing his daily
report. The matter I had come to discuss involved certain inquiries of a military nature, so he was not in
the way. ....

When we had dealt with it, the general asked me
about Panizzardi's telegram which we had just deciphered.

''You are quite sure of the translation you sent us?''

''Yes, quite sure; I am prepared to vouch for every
word.''

The general looked surprised at what I said and
threw the colonel a disconcerted glance. Sandherr, as
imperturbable as if he were under fire, said incisively:

''Dreyfus' treason has been proved. As for the way
in which he worked, if there are still any doubts about
it, the judge-advocate of the Army Council is engaged
in throwing light on it.''

[17] The intelligence service was responsible to General Gonse, one
of the Deputy Chiefs of the General Staff.

Gonse resumed in a firm voice:

"Dreyfus' treason has been proved. We find new evidence daily. . . . Isn't that right, Sandherr?"

Thursday, November 29, 1894

The mystery surrounding the Dreyfus case, the disturbing puzzles that it presents, and finally the inexplicable duration of the preliminary examination are stirring public opinion deeply. People do not understand why, in view of the fact that his guilt is not in doubt and the evidence against him is "striking and shrieks to high heaven," he has not long since been convicted. His co-religionists must obviously be working to save him, they say. But in that case, why does the Minister of War not unmask them? If he is not their dupe, he must obviously be their accomplice!

To calm the excitement, into which a note of anger is creeping, General Mercier has had published in the *Figaro* a long article, obviously written under his inspiration, in which Dreyfus' guilt is presented as an indisputable fact. It says that the General Staff has succeeded in establishing "with absolute certainty" that for three years Dreyfus "had been in contact with agents of a foreign government which was neither the Italian nor the Austro-Hungarian Government." His treasonable activity must, therefore, have been on behalf of Germany.

Count von Münster [18] immediately came to protest

[18] Georg Herbert, Graf von Münster-Ledenburg, born in London in 1820, was Hanoverian Minister in St. Petersburg from 1857 to 1865. After Bismarck's annexation of Hanover in 1866, he threw

against the allegations in this article.

"No official or officer in my Embassy has ever had relations of any kind with Captain Dreyfus," he declared.

He concluded by asking Hanotaux unofficially to deny the "rubbish" in the *Figaro*. Hence the following appeared in the *Temps* last night: "Certain newspapers persist in mentioning accredited embassies in Paris in connection with an espionage case. We are authorized to declare that the allegations concerning them are devoid of all foundation."

Hanotaux sent for me this morning. He looked ill and very uneasy, and his complexion was sallow.

"Are you sure," he asked me abruptly, "are you sure that the letter attributed to Dreyfus was found in the German Embassy?"

"Yes, because I have no reason to doubt the word of Colonel Sandherr, Major Henry, and Captain Lauth. All three have told me that it was found in pieces in Schwartzkoppen's wastepaper basket, and that it reached the General Staff by the 'ordinary route,' that is to say through the woman Bastian."

"Then how do you explain the assurance, the obvious sincerity, with which Münster solemnly assured me that his military attaché has never had any relations with Dreyfus?"

"Schwartzkoppen may have lied to his ambassador or admitted only part of the truth to him. It wouldn't

---

in his lot with Prussia and was successively a Reichstag deputy (1867–73), Ambassador in London, and finally Ambassador in Paris (1885–1900). He died at Hanover in 1902.

have been the first time! There's another possible explanation, which Major Henry suggested to me the other day. Schwartzkoppen may not have had direct relations with Dreyfus but may have served as intermediary for his Brussels colleague, Major von Schmettau.''

''That doesn't solve the problem, because Münster denies any kind of relations with Dreyfus, even indirect.''

''Then I see only one way out: put the question officially to General Mercier.''

''No, certainly not, I shall do nothing of the sort!'' Hanotaux exclaimed with asperity. ''The Dreyfus case does not come within my province; it is purely a matter for the military judicial authorities. . . . General Mercier is involving us in very grave complications indeed. You will remember that I warned him of that on the very first day. Twice I tried to make him listen to reason, to show him the folly of what he was embarking on, but he wouldn't listen to me. And now things have gone too far. . . . Public passions are not released with impunity. . . . As for myself, I have done my duty, the whole of my duty, and my conscience is clear; there is nothing else for me to do. . . . That is why, my dear fellow, I earnestly recommend you to be extremely careful in your relations with the General Staff. Don't take the initiative or make a step, don't even ask any questions, without authority from me.''

''I shall scrupulously observe your instructions.''

Then, as if suddenly rising to the serene level of history, he terminated the interview with these words:

"Believe me, the Dreyfus case is not a mere judicial episode; it will count in our national life . . . and we are still only at the beginning of the crisis."

Sunday, December 9, 1894

The Nationalist newspapers are still implicating the German Embassy in the Dreyfus case, but, to keep their readers' interest from flagging, they are now exploiting a new theme. This is that the mysterious letter found in Schwartzkoppen's papers is of such gravity that, *if its contents were divulged, it might lead to anything;* that the Government has, therefore, decided to destroy it; that the overwhelming case against Dreyfus is thus reduced to mere suspicion, and Israel is about to triumph! . . . . However, the assurance is simultaneously given that General Mercier, who has long since ferreted out the Judaeo-German plot, has taken care to have the damning letter photographed. Let the valets of Germany and the traitor's accomplices beware! . . . .

On top of this, by an unhappy coincidence, the semi-official newspapers announce that the Foreign Minister has fallen ill. Nothing could be better calculated to lend color to the fantastic and preposterous story circulated in millions of copies by the militarist press.

Hanotaux has indeed fallen ill; he has influenza, with lung and liver complications. Any lively emotion, any strong vexation, automatically gives him liver trouble; he was thus *a priori* in a bad state to resist an influenza infection.

He is worried by his condition, which is serious. Accordingly, before he took to his bed, he gave Nisard a sealed envelope containing an account of all he did to dissuade General Mercier from having Dreyfus charged. Nisard handed the envelope over to me, and I immediately put it in one of my safes.

Thursday, December 13, 1894

The Nationalist press persists with the story that Hanotaux went secretly to the German Embassy to hand back to Count von Münster the mysterious letter that disclosed the Jew's crime.

This absurd legend, which is coming more and more to be believed, seems to be unacceptable to German opinion. ''An Imperial Embassy does not exist for the purpose of providing material for the serial novels of the French press.''

Late yesterday afternoon Count von Münster came and protested to Nisard about the objectionable polemics in which certain newspapers persist in involving his embassy. The old aristocrat, courteous and moderate as usual, did not disguise the fact that he was rather tired of having to repeat his complaints so often. Nisard could promise him only another note to the Havas agency. Münster asked that it should at least be very precise, and that it should be submitted to him first.

In Hanotaux's absence Révoil, his principal private secretary, drafted it with Nisard. It was as follows:

''Statements to the effect that the Minister of Foreign Affairs has returned to the German Ambassador any document of any kind referring either to the Dreyfus case or to any acts of espionage are totally incorrect.''

The draft was submitted during the evening to Count von Münster, who declared himself fully satisfied with it.

In view of the possibility that the Ambassador might have demanded something more explicit, Charles Dupuy, the Prime Minister, had asked General Mercier, Nisard, and Révoil to join him at the Élysée Palace at ten o'clock. They had only just arrived when the official who had been sent to the German Embassy came to tell them that Münster had accepted the draft without reservations. It was put out by the Havas agency at 11:30.[19]

Sunday, December 16, 1894

As was to be expected, the statement that the Government caused to be put out three days ago by the Havas agency at Count von Münster's request was re-

---

[19] *Author's note:* By a strange distortion of memory, this slight incident became, four years later, in General Mercier's memoir *la Nuit historique:* "From eight o'clock in the evening until half-past twelve, I remained with M. Charles Dupuy in the office of the President of the Republic, waiting to hear whether war or peace was going to emerge from the telegrams being exchanged between the Kaiser and Count von Münster. Meanwhile, at the Ministry of War, General de Boisdeffre, surrounded by his officers, was holding himself ready to give the order for mobilization." It should be noted that General Mercier must have been guilty of gross negligence in this hour of supreme peril as Saussier, the Commander-in-Chief, spent the evening quietly by his own fireside and was warned of nothing.

ceived with complete incredulity by the enlightened
apostles of the Nationalist creed. But their incredulity
is never negative. Whenever they are inconveniently
contradicted, they respond by producing an imaginary
fact. The new fable that they are now spreading to the
four winds is that "the mysterious letter, whose return the German Ambassador demanded under an
oath of eternal secrecy, would prove the intervention
in Dreyfus' treason of no less a personage than the
Kaiser himself."

And to say that a mind as subtle and acute as that
of Maurice Barrès should fall for such rubbish! Yesterday, while dining at the house of a lady who later
told me the story, he announced peremptorily: "There
lies the whole explanation of the Dreyfus case!" [20]

Tuesday, December 18, 1894

I called on Mme Casimir-Perier senior, who has just
returned to Paris, and found her son with her.

We talked about the Dreyfus case. Casimir-Perier

[20] Maurice Barrès had been Boulangist deputy for Nancy from
1889 to 1893. From September, 1894, to March, 1895, he edited the
Cocarde, a Nationalist newspaper which he founded, and then
worked for the *Patrie* and the *Journal;* he attended the Rennes
court-martial on behalf of the latter. In 1897 he published *les Déra-
cinés,* the first volume of his *Roman de l'énergie nationale,* which
demonstrated the place that political preoccupations had assumed in
his mind. In 1899 he became one of the founders and leaders of the
League of the French Fatherland, which was formed in opposition
to the League of the Rights of Man by opponents of the reopening
of the Dreyfus case. His reports and memories of the case provided
the material for the second and most voluminous of his *Scènes et
doctrines du nationalisme,* published in 1902.

told me that two or three days ago he received Bertillon, the head of the anthropometric service at the Préfecture of Police, who has been called on to give an expert opinion on the handwriting of the *bordereau* and declares categorically that he recognizes in it the handwriting of Captain Dreyfus.

"Do you know this Bertillon?" he asked me.

"Yes, slightly. We sometimes ask him to photograph secret documents."

"What do you think of him?"

"He is highly thought of at the Préfecture of Police; he is said to be very clever, very ingenious, but rather odd."

"Odd?" Casimir-Perier exclaimed. "Odd? He's not odd; he's mad! And mad in such an extraordinary, cabalistic way that I am still completely overwhelmed by him. He spent three hours proving to me that Dreyfus himself imitated his own handwriting to write the *bordereau,* and he used such unintelligible jargon, talked such grotesque gibberish, and emphasized each one of his statements by such strange looks, that I thought I was in the presence of a lunatic escaped from the Salpétrière or Villejuif!"

Casimir-Perier also told me that at a shoot at Marly last week, Saussier, the Commander-in-Chief, said to him: "Dreyfus is not guilty. That fool Mercier has put his finger in his own eye again!"

"Then why is the Commander-in-Chief having Dreyfus court-martialed?"

"That's exactly what I asked him, but he said that the report of the examining officer did not permit him to act otherwise, and besides, what did it matter, because the court-martial would decide."

Saturday, December 22, 1894

The court-martial, after long deliberation, has unanimously declared Dreyfus guilty of treason and sentenced him to "perpetual deportation in a fortified place" as well as to military degradation.

I heard the news at ten minutes past seven, just as I was preparing to leave the office. Almost simultaneously, a telephone call summoned me to the Élysée.

Casimir-Perier received me in his dressing-room, where he was finishing dressing for dinner.

"Well," he said, "so it's over! I shan't conceal from you that a terrible load has been taken off my mind by the unanimity of the verdict because, after all, these officers are fine, honest, scrupulous men. They certainly would not convict one of their comrades, even a Jew, unless they were convinced by unquestionable evidence of his guilt. . . . What were they convinced by? On that I no longer know what to think; I am the more puzzled because the Prefect of Police came to see me just now, while the court was still considering its verdict, and told me that he believed there was going to be an acquittal. . . . What is your impression?"

"I have the same impression as you, Mr. President. The unanimity of the verdict shows the certainty in the minds of the members of the court; we can only accept their verdict; they evidently had knowledge of things that I have not."

Sunday, December 23, 1894

There is only one note in the comment on the verdict this morning throughout the whole of the Paris press, from the extreme Right to the extreme Left, from the clerical and Monarchist journals to the organs of the most extreme Socialism: approval, relief, satisfaction, joy—a triumphant, vindictive, ferocious joy.

Being curious to know what the provincial newspapers said, late this afternoon I went to the Quai d'Orsay where I asked for the telegraphic summary of the departmental press. It struck the same note, a fierce, tumultuous joy, as if we had just escaped from a great national danger. I thought of the frenzied cheerfulness of Rome when it heard the news of Cleopatra's death:

> *Nunc est bibendum, nunc pede libero*
> *Pulsanda tellus. . . .*

There is no doubt about it; the French conscience has been profoundly stirred.

But Dreyfus' conviction has surprised no one; it can even be said that in everyone's eyes, he was convicted by the mere fact of having been accused. One of the most violent of the Nationalist swashbucklers acutely foresaw this mentality of the crowd when at the beginning of the preliminary investigation he wrote: "If it is proved that the Minister of War has cast opprobrium on the army without irrefutable proofs; in a word, if Captain Dreyfus is acquitted, it is General

Mercier who becomes the traitor.'' Thus the conviction
came to look like a mere procedural detail, the consequence implicit in the charge.

But what was unexpected, what even the ranters of
the *Libre Parole* had not dared to hope for, was a
unanimous verdict.

Thus the most scrupulous were able to rejoice without fear, for seven officers would not have convicted a
comrade, a brother-in-arms, even if he were a Jew,
without striking proof of his guilt.

In any case, the commotion into which the country
has been plunged can be easily enough explained. The
monstrousness of the crime, France's love of her army,
the stain cast on the flag, the social rank of the accused, the melodramatic circumstances, the secret maneuvers of Jewry to save the traitor, the threatening
attitude of Germany, the terrible secret that hovered
over the Kaiser's personal role—less than all this
would have sufficed to exalt people's imaginations and
fill them with fanaticism.

Monday, December 24, 1894

The German Chancellery has caused the following to
be published through the Wolff agency:

*French newspapers, in spite of a number of official
denials, continue to involve the German Embassy in
the Dreyfus case. It is asserted, in particular, that
Count von Münster has made secret representations
arising out of a document abstracted from the Em-*

bassy. An authoritative source enables it once more to be stated explicitly that all these allegations are pure inventions and constitute an audacious attempt to conceal the truth. The German Embassy has never had the slightest contact with Dreyfus, either direct or indirect, and hence there can be no question of any document emanating from Dreyfus or of any attempts at a secret deal.

Tuesday, December 25, 1894

Hanotaux's health is improving so slowly that the doctors have ordered him to the Côte d'Azur for some weeks, so he is leaving for Cannes tomorrow.

According to what I have been told by one of the few who see him, he is as depressed mentally as he is physically. The Dreyfus case haunts him; he is unable to see to the bottom of it. In the statement given to the Wolff agency yesterday by the German Chancellery, he was struck by the peremptory tone with which the Imperial Government repudiated responsibility for the Dreyfus affair while denouncing the allegations in the French press as an *audacious attempt to conceal the truth.*

Nisard, who excels in the analysis and dissection of documents, had hit on this phrase immediately. He pointed it out to me this morning.

"The whole interest, the whole substance, of the statement is concentrated in that phrase," he said. "In Berlin they know the truth; but they don't tell us. Some individuals in Paris know it too, but they don't tell us either."

"Obviously there is something mysterious here because we are faced with two irreconcilable statements. On the one hand, the document that led to Dreyfus' conviction was found among Schwartzkoppen's papers; on the other, Schwartzkoppen never had any dealings with Dreyfus."

After long, silent reflection, Nisard went on:

"To see clearly in the matter, one would have to have in one's hands the file that caused the court-martial to convict . . . and it would have to be studied closely, under a magnifying glass!"

Wednesday, December 26, 1894

Hanotaux is leaving for Cannes in a few minutes' time. Münster came to see him this afternoon and said to him anxiously:

"Shall we ever know what is at the bottom of the Dreyfus case?"

Hanotaux was unwilling to accept battle on this terrain.

"The verdict of the court-martial has ended the Dreyfus case," he said. "I no longer have any right to discuss it."

Thursday, December 27, 1894

The peremptory Wolff agency statement must have caused a sensation at the General Staff, for Colonel Sandherr came to see me this afternoon, bringing me some unimportant papers as an excuse. After the first sentence he said to me in his loud, gruff voice:

"What does this Wolff agency statement mean?
What is in store for us now? When are these b . . .
Germans going to keep their mouths shut? Do we dis-
cuss the verdicts of their courts-martial?"

I impartially stated the facts. I pointed out that
the Wolff agency had not discussed the court-mar-
tial verdict, but had confined itself to stating that
Schwartzkoppen had never had any dealings with
Dreyfus and that the *bordereau* had not come from the
German Embassy.

"Well, it lies on both points!" Sandherr said.

"You have information on the matter that I lack," I
answered. "So far as I am concerned, there is much
about the case that remains impenetrable and obscure,
and I have no alternative but to rely on you."

"I assure you that the court had not the slightest
doubt about Dreyfus' guilt; and I also assure you that
if you had been a member of the court you would have
come to the same decision as they. . . . Don't ask me
any more; I am bound to secrecy."

"Calm yourself, my dear colonel. You have instructions to tell me nothing, and I have instructions to ask
you nothing."

He burst into a hearty laugh, lighted a cigarette, and
started telling me stories about some of the external
circumstances of the court-martial.

"I wasn't in court," he said, "but I was kept informed from hour to hour by Major Picquart,[21] Major

[21] Marie Georges Picquart, born at Strasbourg in 1854, entered
St. Cyr in 1872 and subsequently attended the Staff College. In
1885 he was attached to General de Courcy's staff in the operations

Henry,[22] and Captain Lauth,[23] who kept bobbing back
and forth between the courtroom and the War Ministry.''

Here are the pictures and impressions that remain
in my mind as the result of what he told me.

First, the prisoner. Face unpleasant, eyes short-
sighted and deceitful, voice dry, toneless, metallic, ''a
voice of zinc.'' Being unable to refute any of the overwhelming charges against him, he had even denied the
evidence. Bertillon's expert evidence had disconcerted
him completely; while listening to it, he had trembled
in all his limbs; he had looked as if he were saying to
himself: Now I'm done for!

Next, the lawyer. Demange was an ''unpleasant,
very unpleasant character'' who had made a specialty

---

in Tonkin and on the Chinese frontier. He became a major at the
age of thirty-three and an instructor in topography at the École
de Guerre and succeeded Colonel Sandherr as head of the intelligence
department on July 1, 1895.

[22] Hubert Joseph Henry, born at Pogny (Marne) in 1846, came
of a farming family and joined the army in the ranks in 1865. In
the 1870 war he was a sergeant-major and was made prisoner twice,
but escaped; his conduct under fire caused him to be commissioned
in the field. In 1876 he became aide-de-camp to General de Miribel
and in 1877 was assigned to the intelligence service. He took part as
a captain in the campaigns in Tunisia (1882) and Tonkin (1887).
In 1891 he was promoted to major and was again assigned to the
intelligence service on January 13, 1893, and became Colonel Sandherr's immediate subordinate. He was promoted to lieutenant-colonel
in 1897.

[23] Jules Lauth, born at Saverne in 1858, after service with various
cavalry units was transferred to the intelligence service on August
12, 1893, with the rank of captain. His special task was the translation of German documents. He was promoted to major in 1897
and retired in 1906.

of defending spies; he was in the hands of the Jews. "At the intelligence department we have a file on him that might take him a long way!"

I pointed out to Sandherr that Maître Demange was a fervent Catholic, that his wife was a general's daughter, and that, moreover, he enjoyed a high reputation among his colleagues. "I don't give a damn for all that," Sandherr said. "I know what I know!"

Now for the witnesses for the prosecution. Among these the chief role had been played by Major du Paty de Clam, who had conducted the preliminary examination, and Major Henry, who appeared as the representative of intelligence service by order of General de Boisdeffre. Du Paty de Clam had showed himself "as firm and lucid as he was tenacious," but at times his vanity, his arrogance, his need always to play a star role, irritated the court. Henry, however, had been admirable, both in coolness and in precision; "all his words carried like bullets." With one hand on the crucifix and the other pointing at Dreyfus, he had declared: "By my soul and conscience, I swear that the traitor is there!" Then it was as if he had pronounced the sentence himself.

Finally, Colonel Maurel, the presiding officer, had been "beyond all praise." As soon as the proceedings opened, he had made it clear that they would be conducted in proper military fashion. He had put Demange in his place straight away; two or three times he had interrupted him, and in such an abrupt tone that he had piped down until the end of the trial. Maurel was equally magnificent with the witnesses for the defense. Thus, on the third day, "an ugly-looking Jew" had been seen advancing toward the bar. "What is your name?" Maurel had asked him. "My name is Dreyfus; I am the Chief Rabbi of Paris." "What do you know about the case?" "I know nothing about the case, but I have known the prisoner's family for a long time, and I consider them a very honest family." "Very well, you can withdraw!" "I tell you old Maurel presided marvelously!" Sandherr went on, with a click of the tongue. I timidly pointed out that, after all, one could not reproach a chief rabbi for looking like a Jew, and that if Dreyfus, instead of being a Jew, had been a Catholic, Sandherr would have found it perfectly natural if the Archbishop of Paris had come forward to give evidence—what was known as evidence of character—about his antecedents and family. But Sandherr remained imperturbable and answered with a sneer:

"That doesn't alter the fact that old Maurel presided marvelously!"

Saturday, January 5, 1895

The "execution" parade took place at forty-five minutes past eight, in the great court of the École Militaire, which was full of troops. In accordance with the provision of the military penal code, a detachment had been sent by every regiment of the Paris garrison.

I was present at the ceremony, in the uniform of a lieutenant of artillery; Colonel Sandherr allowed me to join his officers.

The morning was icy. Every now and then a sharp, biting wind blew big flakes of snow into our faces; it was a sinister setting under the pale sky.

Outside the gate, in the Place de Fontenoy, an enormous crowd, contained with difficulty by the police, was chafing, fidgeting, whistling, and shouting: "Death to the Jews!" "Death to the traitor!" "Death to Judas!"

Nine o'clock struck. General Darras, on horseback, followed by his staff, drew his sword. There was a roll of drums. "Attention! Shoulder arms!"

In a terrifying silence, in which these thousands of men seemed to be holding their breath, Dreyfus appeared at the right corner of the court, in the midst of a corporal and four gunners, with saber in hand and revolver on his belt. He advanced firmly, head high, looking as if he were in command of his escort.

He was marched before General Darras, where he stopped, heels together, standing at attention. The escort retired four paces.

The general rose in his stirrups and, holding his sword aloft, said:

"Alfred Dreyfus, you are no longer worthy to carry arms. In the name of the French people, we degrade you!"

A warrant officer of the Garde républicaine, a giant of a man, Sergeant-Major Bouxin, approached the condemned man as he stood there motionless and, with angry gestures, tore off the braid from his cap and sleeves, the buttons from his jacket, his shoulder-straps, all his marks of rank, and threw them in the mud. When Dreyfus' uniform had been reduced to tatters, the giant took his saber and scabbard and broke them over his knee. The fearful ordeal seemed interminable. I said to Sandherr, who had placed me on his left: "How can a man submit to such humiliation? It seems to me that if I were in his skin and were innocent, I should revolt, struggle, shout!" Sandherr replied with a ferocious grin: "It's obvious that you don't know the Jews! That race has neither patriotism, nor honor, nor pride. For centuries, they have done nothing but betray. Remember that they betrayed Christ!"

When the giant had completed his revolting task, Dreyfus shouted: "You have just degraded an innocent man. By the head of my wife and my children, I swear that I am innocent!"

Now for the last act of the drama.

Dreyfus, in tatters, looking as grotesque as pitiable, of his own accord stepped back between his escort. He was then marched the whole length of the lined-up detachments, which was a long way, for at least four thousand men were on parade.

During this Calvary, Dreyfus did not for one moment falter or revolt. His pace was as firm and rhythmical as that of his gunner escorts. Twice I heard him shout: "I am innocent!"

Finally he passed in front of our group. In a dry, toneless, mechanical voice, in which there was not a trace of emotion, he again shouted: "I am innocent!"

When he reached the end of the courtyard, two *gendarmes* seized him, handcuffed him, and put him in a Black Maria, which trotted quickly away.

The drama was over; but no, it was not entirely over. The author of the military penal code had felt that an epilogue was necessary to avoid leaving the troops with a demoralizing impression.

So, as soon as the Black Maria had left the court, a magnificent command rang out: "Attention! The parade will march past! Columns, right! . . . ."

General Darras raised his sword; the drums beat, the bugles sounded, the band struck up the *Sambre-et-Meuse*. While the troops marched past at a lively pace, I felt as if delivered from a horrible oppression, a fearful nightmare. The air suddenly seemed pure and healthy. The cheerful *Sambre-et-Meuse* march seemed to say: Forget the hideous dream! Up with your hearts! France still lives!

I reached the Foreign Ministry at ten o'clock. I went to warm myself with a cup of tea in Nisard's room; Nisard was impatient to hear about the degradation ceremony. I described it in detail and concluded:

"If I had any doubts about Dreyfus' guilt during the judicial proceedings, I no longer have them now. In my opinion his behavior at the 'execution parade' was sufficient to convict him. To have lent himself so docilely, so passively to such a torture, the man must be devoid of moral sensibility. Not a gesture of revolt, not a cry of horror, not a tear, not a murmur! True, he protested his innocence several times, but all his protestations sounded false; there was no warmth in them; his voice might have been the voice of an automaton."

Nisard remained silent for some time, his eyes halfclosed. Then, with the subtle intuition that has so often struck me, he said:

"We shall hear about this Jew again. . . . After all, he has been convicted on a vague similarity of handwriting, for the secret documents that convinced the court-martial of his guilt don't count, they are rubbish. Remember what Tacitus said about courts-martial: *Castrensis jurisdictio obtusa.*"

Sunday, January 6, 1895

Nisard telephoned me at nine o'clock this morning. "Come and see me at once!" he said.

"There's news," he told me when I reached his flat, "and news that is not without gravity, for now the Kaiser has entered the scene."

He described the situation that had arisen. He foresaw various possible courses of action that might be taken to deal with it, but before making up his mind, he wanted some definite information that he thought I was in a position to give him.

Late yesterday afternoon, then, the German Ambassador had asked to be received officially by Charles Dupuy, the Prime Minister, who is acting as Foreign Minister in Hanotaux's absence. Dupuy received him immediately, and the Ambassador informed him that the Emperor was offended by the slanderous references that the French press persisted in making against his Embassy and had instructed him to demand from the President of the Republic a peremptory denial of these accusations. He simultaneously handed to Charles Dupuy the translation of a telegram that the Imperial Chancellor, Prince Hohenlohe, had just sent him:

H.M. the Emperor, having full confidence in the good faith of the President and Government of the Republic, requests Your Excellency to inform M. Casimir-Perier that if it is proved that the German Embassy has in no way been implicated in the Dreyfus case, His Majesty hopes that the Government of the Republic will not hesitate to announce it.

Without this formal declaration, the legends that the French press continues to propagate would persist and compromise the position of the Emperor's representative.

(*signed*) HOHENLOHE [24]

In the course of the conversation that followed the handing over of this telegram, the Ambassador said:

"If my Embassy is in any way involved in the Dreyfus case, let us be told so, and we shall take the neces-

[24] Chlodwig, Prince von Hohenlohe-Schillingsfürst (1819–1901), had, before the establishment of the German Empire, been Foreign Minister and subsequently Prime Minister of the Kingdom of Bavaria. Under the new Empire, he was in turn deputy president of the Reichstag (1871–73), German Ambassador in Paris (1873–85), and Governor of Alsace-Lorraine (1885–94). He succeeded Caprivi as Chancellor in October, 1894, and remained Chancellor until October, 1900.

sary punitive measures. But if it is not involved, let it
be publicly stated.''

The Prime Minister reported immediately to Casimir-Perier, who arranged to receive Münster at half-
past one this afternoon.

Hanotaux, who was informed by telegram yesterday
evening, replied: ''I am of the opinion that there
should be a frank talk with the German Ambassador.''
He also announced that he was returning immediately.

Nisard went on:

''I think our Minister is right. The President of the
Republic must talk to the German Ambassador with
complete frankness, without dissimulating anything
of the truth.... But, in your opinion, what is the truth,
the real truth?''

''Sir, you talk to me like Pontius Pilate. What is
truth? I know the official truth; I fear that there may
be another.''

''Does that other truth, which I shall call the *real*
truth, in your opinion imply that Dreyfus is innocent?''

''I have several times wondered whether he might
not be innocent. But today, after the unanimous verdict
of the court-martial, and particularly after the shameful fashion in which he submitted to his degradation, I
no longer have doubts about his guilt.''

''And so?''

''And so, sir, I imagine—but it is a mere hypothesis
—I imagine that the verdict of the court-martial was
based on evidence that I do not know, that I do not
even suspect, and that that evidence cannot or dare not

be publicly admitted because it comes from a source that cannot be admitted.''

''So the nearest to the truth would be the fables in the Nationalist press?''

''No, because, in my opinion, what cannot be admitted is not the evidence itself, but what authenticates it, that is to say its source; I mean the expedients and stratagems by which our intelligence services abstracted it from the German Embassy. Sandherr's agents are capable of the maddest schemes, the most dangerous acts of temerity. . . . In this connection there is a formidable precedent that could be quoted. If I am not mistaken, it was in 1891—you remember how bad our relations with Britain were at that time because of Siam. To gain information Sandherr took into his pay the valet of the Ambassador, Lord Lytton. You also remember that Lytton [25] was a neurotic, who sometimes took champagne to keep himself going and sometimes took drugs to enable him to sleep. In either case he slept very soundly. Every night before going to bed he put the letters and telegrams of the day in a drawer, the key of which, a small golden key strung on a curbchain, never left him. He used carefully to put it on his night table, with his watch chain. As soon as he was asleep, the valet would creep into his room, take the key, open the drawer, and remove the papers. Then

[25] Edward Robert Bulwer Lytton, first Earl of Lytton (1831–91), was the son of Lord Lytton, the author of *The Last Days of Pompeii*. He served in the diplomatic service and from 1876 to 1880 was Viceroy of India. He was appointed Ambassador in Paris in 1887 and died there in 1891. He wrote poems and novels under the name of Owen Meredith.

he quickly took them to a house in the Rue d'Aguesseau, where an officer of the intelligence department, Captain Rollin, would be waiting for him. An hour later the papers and golden key would be back in their place. But you can imagine the manner in which the British Government would have demanded redress if it had discovered this violation of human rights, carried out at night, and in the Ambassador's own bedroom, and with the connivance of an officer in service into the bargain. In fact Lord Lytton must have ended by noticing something, because one day he suddenly gave his valet the sack, without giving him any explanation. . . . Well! If the evidence that establishes Dreyfus' guilt reached the General Staff in circumstances as compromising to the French Government as that, you will appreciate that it is impossible to have such dirty linen washed in public. . . . But, I repeat, all this is mere hypothesis, based on nothing positive whatsoever.''

Nisard thought for a few moments, picked up his pen, scribbled two or three lines as if he were searching for a formula, and then said:

"Obviously there is a mystery about where the *bordereau* came from. It was not abstracted from the Embassy in the way we were told. Münster has never ceased to repeat that the letter attributed to Dreyfus could not have been discovered in his Embassy because it was never received there. The President of the Republic will, therefore, be well advised to avoid as far as possible all discussion of where the *bordereau* came from. That being the case, what would you say if M.

Casimir-Perier, to reconcile the position of our General Staff with that of the German Embassy, used a formula of the following nature? 'An anonymous document, damning for Dreyfus, was found in your Embassy; we know that for a fact. But we do not impute to you any responsibility for receiving that document, any more than the Imperial Government would dream of holding us responsible for the papers brought to us from Germany, for of course you realize that such papers are brought us.' This formula would, in my opinion, have the double advantage of repudiating all German involvement in Dreyfus' crime while being in perfect harmony with the General Staff case as presented to the court-martial.''

''Perfect! Your predecessor, M. d'Hauterive, Talleyrand's favorite disciple, would not have thought of anything better.''

Nisard, thereupon, dismissed me to go and see the Prime Minister.

Just when I reached my office, a telephone call came from the Élysée to say that the President of the Republic invited me to dine with him *en famille* at his mother's this evening, but that, if I were not free, he would be glad if I went to see him at six o'clock. Having myself invited some friends to dinner this evening, I replied that I should not fail to be at the Élysée at six o'clock.

A stormy atmosphere was evident as soon as I entered the President's office. His desk was bare—not a letter, not a book, not a newspaper, not even a sheet of paper was to be seen. Casimir-Perier, with flashing eyes and indignation written on his face, was striding rapidly up and down with long, jerky footsteps which made him turn sharply on himself at each end of the room.

In sharp, ringing tones he said:

"I wanted to tell you this very day about my conversation with the German Ambassador, because it is impossible to say what may happen tomorrow, and I have every confidence in you. . . . But first of all, my dear fellow, let me tell you that your great Minister, M. Hanotaux, has put me in the most embarrassing, the most false, the most humiliating position in which a chief of state could possibly find himself.

"I learned to my astonishment that Münster had been to see him five or six times to protest officially against the indictment of Dreyfus; one day he even offered to have a full and frank discussion of the mysterious affair. Now, Hanotaux never informed me of these grave conversations. He never mentioned them to me.

"The result was that when Münster brought up this or that of his statements, I did not know what to reply; I was mortified. . . . You will admit that on this occasion M. Hanotaux has treated me in a rather cavalier, not to say shameless, fashion. I may add that if I had been aware of the reiterated statements of the German Chancellery, I should not have failed to refer the matter to the Council of Ministers, and I do not doubt that things would have taken a different course. But this fashion of ignoring me, of diminishing my role and discrediting it, is obviously part of a system. They are

trying to push me to extremes, and they will succeed
... perhaps sooner than they think!''

In the way he spoke, I could feel the quivering of his
old hatred of the ''perfidious and presumptuous Hanotaux''; his bitter disgust with politics; his resentment
at having allowed himself to be shut up in the Élysée—
''this bogus setting in which one does nothing but receive blows without being able to return them''; his
pain at the abominable insults with which the Socialist
newspapers torment him, aiming their shafts at his
illustrious ancestor, the so-called ''great usurer of
Grenoble,'' and thus wounding his family pride; and
finally, his worst suffering, a terrible, devouring, and
secret passion which gnaws at him like a cancer. After
this vigorous exordium, he read me a memorandum in
which he described his conversation with Münster; he
actually asked me to take a copy to keep for myself. It
begins as follows:

*I said to the Ambassador that Prince von Hohen-
lohe's telegram had rather surprised me, and that it
was rather unusual, as it made a direct appeal to the
President of the Republic, almost to his good faith as a
private individual. I explained that, out of respect for
our Constitution, I ought perhaps to have declined the
conversation and asked the Ambassador to confer with
the Prime Minister. But my memory of my previous
relations with Count von Münster, my esteem for him,
my desire to facilitate his task, would cause me to accept a conversation with him that I should refuse to
anyone else. . . .*

Then, coming to the crux of the matter, Casimir-Perier very skillfully developed the argument suggested by Nisard.

We know for a fact that the anonymous letter, now known as the bordereau, *was found at your place of residence. But there is nothing to show that the document was solicited. Your Embassy is therefore no more responsible for having received it than we are for the papers that are brought to us from Germany. . . .*

Münster accepted this explanation in principle, but categorically insisted that the *bordereau* did not come from his Embassy.

In conclusion, the President and the Ambassador agreed on the general lines of a statement to be put out by the Havas agency, and they parted on very friendly terms.

From the Élysée, Münster went to the Place Beauvau to draft the statement with the Prime Minister; the Ambassador then immediately telegraphed it to Berlin.

Wednesday, January 9, 1895

Following the German Ambassador's conversation with the President of the Republic, the Berlin Chancellery has approved the following statement, which has just been sent to the Havas agency: "Since the conviction of the former Captain Dreyfus, certain newspapers, in various articles relating to espionage, persist in implicating foreign embassies and legations in Paris.

We are authorized to state that the allegations concerning them are devoid of all foundation."

Sunday, January 13, 1895

I dined with Mme Casimir-Perier senior, with the President of the Republic, and friends of the family. Among the guests were the Prefect of Police, Lépine, and the Military Governor of Paris, General Saussier, the Commander-in-Chief.

All through dinner I was struck by Casimir-Perier's depressed and baleful appearance, his absent, staring eyes, his pallor, his drooping figure. Throughout the meal, he did not speak a word. I felt sure he was pondering about his mad idea of resigning. Nobody dared interrupt his silence. Every now and then his old mother glanced sharply at him across the table, as if to tell him to pull himself together. We all felt most uncomfortable.

In the drawing-room after dinner, before the coffee was served, General Saussier drew Lépine and me aside.

"You noticed the President's face," he said. "What has happened?"

"So far as home politics are concerned," the Prefect of Police replied, "nothing, except for the Cabinet dissensions you know about, which might well lead to its resignation. But in any case, nothing serious."

Saussier turned to me.

"And foreign politics? Is the German Ambassador

by any chance trying to reopen discussion of the Dreyfus case?''

"Certainly not. The incident that led to Münster's
démarche a week ago is closed. M. Casimir-Perier ex-
tricated us very skillfully from an awkward situation.
There's no more question of it.''

"Is it true," Lépine asked, "that one day, or rather
one night, we were on the brink of war?''

Saussier fixed him with his large, malicious eyes.

"Your question amazes me, my dear Prefect. Only
the readers of the *Libre Parole* could believe such
twaddle. M. Casimir-Perier and M. Dupuy have described their conversations with Count von Münster
to me, and I assure you all passed off very calmly and
courteously.''

I confirmed what the Commander-in-Chief said, and
we rejoined the other guests.

Two or three times during the evening I tried to
make an opportunity to talk to M. Casimir-Perier
alone, but he did not lend himself to it.

At about half-past ten everybody left. Mme Jean
Casimir-Perier took me aside.

"Since your last visit to the Élysée, Casimir's frame
of mind has got still worse. I fear he may do something
impulsive. I am terribly sad. Come to see us soon!''

Wednesday, January 16, 1895

At eight o'clock this morning my servant came into my
room with a look of consternation on his face.

"Have you heard the news, sir?"

"No."

"President Casimir-Perier has gone!"

Unfortunately, this was true. In spite of the expostulations of his Ministers, his mother, his wife, his sister, his brother-in-law Ségur, his old friend Félix de Bourquenay, and I do not dare also say myself, he resigned last night; and this grave decision, for which the official reasons seem all the more insignificant because the real reason is not even suspected, will be put down as the whim of a spoiled child, an evasion, a flight!

Friday, January 18, 1895

The congress [26] met yesterday at Versailles. After two hours of voting, Félix Faure was proclaimed President of the Republic. Once more the mechanism of the Constitution—this Republican Constitution enacted by a Monarchist assembly—worked with perfect smoothness and efficiency.

The new President, who held the portfolio of the Colonies in the reign of Casimir-Perier, is intelligent, honest, and likable. Moreover he has good health, good nature, and a good figure, in which he shows some satisfaction. He comes of very modest origins, having started in life as a tanner's laborer. He, therefore, deserves all the more credit for having become what he is today, that is to say, a man of enlightened understand-

[26] That is, a joint session of the Senate and Chamber of Deputies.

ing, careful judgment, wide experience, and irreproachable manners.[27]

During the night Dreyfus left with a trainload of
convicts for La Rochelle and the Île de Ré, from where
he will soon embark for French Guiana. He is to serve
his sentence in one of the three islands of Salut, opposite Cayenne. This island, which is bare, rocky, and
scorching, has hitherto been reserved for convict
lepers. Its very name sounds sinister; it is Devil's Island.

[27] Félix Faure, born in Paris in 1841, was the son of a cabinet-
maker. After starting as a tanner's laborer, he set up a skin-dressing
shop at Havre, which prospered. He became deputy mayor of
Havre, was elected deputy for that town in 1881, and was subsequently constantly re-elected. He became Under-Secretary of State
for Commerce in the Gambetta Cabinet (1881), was Minister of
Marine and Minister for the Colonies in Jules Ferry's Cabinet
(1883–85), and Minister for the Colonies in the Tirard Cabinet
(1888). He became deputy president of the Chamber in 1893, was
Minister of Marine in the Dupuy Cabinet (1894–95), and was elected
President of the Republic on January 17, 1895.

2. FIRST RAYS OF LIGHT

2. FIRST RAYS OF LIGHT

From Monday, June 1, to Wednesday, July 1, 1896

As an accident to my leg did not permit me as usual to take my annual training as a reserve officer with the horse artillery of the 5th Cavalry Division, I was assigned for a month to the information service.

For the past year Lieutenant-Colonel Picquart has taken the place of Colonel Sandherr, who is dying of general paralysis. The deputy chief of the service is no longer Major Cordier, who has been promoted to lieutenant-colonel and assigned to the 41st Regiment of Infantry at Rennes; he has been succeeded by Major Henry. Next in order are Captains Lauth, Junck, and Valdant, and then the irremovable archivist Gribelin. To complete the picture, I also note two officials of the

Sûreté Générale, Police Superintendents Desvernine and Tomps.

Picquart is an interesting figure; and how different from his predecessor, the cunning and crude *gendarme* Sandherr!

He is aged forty-six, was mentioned in dispatches for brilliant feats of arms in the Tonkin campaign, is a former instructor at the École de Guerre, and enjoys the high esteem of General Galliffet. He is tall, slender, elegant, possesses good judgment and a keen and caustic intelligence, all of which he generally conceals behind a distant and reserved manner. For the official relations between us since he has been in charge of the intelligence service, I have nothing but praise.

To pass the time of my term, he first gave me some theoretical work to do, such as working out a clandestine relay system in certain neutral countries in order to assure communication in wartime between the General Staff and its secret sources of information.

But soon I was given better work to do, namely acting as intermediary between Hanotaux and General de Boisdeffre in preparation for the great event that is still a tremendous secret, namely, the forthcoming visit of the Emperor Nicholas and the Empress Alexandra to the President of the Republic. The way for this visit was very skillfully prepared by Boisdeffre during the recent coronation celebrations in Moscow, and for another month it will not be entirely certain that it is coming off because of the numerous engagements that the Czar has already more or less accepted for the summer. Nevertheless President Faure desires

a detailed memorandum to be submitted to him as soon
as possible on Franco-Russian relations during recent
months and on the possible application of the alliance
to the great eastern problems. I have been charged
with this work.

Intelligence work, which I have never seen so closely
before, hardly justifies the romantic and fascinating
reputation that it enjoys from afar. I do not hold
against it the fact that it is generally dirty and dis-
gusting and full of impostures and deceits, for it is
that, so to speak, by its very nature. But what de-
prives it of all its glamor and poetry in my eyes is that
it is carried out by officers. Alfred de Vigny did not
foresee this low form of *servitude militaire*. Why are
our espionage systems not transferred to the Ministry of the Interior? The General Staff would retain
responsibility for inspiring inquiries and appraising
the results.

Moreover, things do not seem to have been going
very well in the intelligence department. I no longer
found the happy-family atmosphere that prevailed
there in Sandherr's time. I have several times felt that
the chief of the department and his colleagues were at
loggerheads. One evening, for instance, when I left the
Ministry with Henry and he took me to the Champs-
Élysées on the pretext of "stretching our legs a bit,"
he suddenly said to me, with a note of bitterness that I
had not heard him use before:

"Well! Do you realize that we regret Sandherr?
What side this Picquart puts on! And then, if you

knew what a bad egg he is. . . . But let's talk about something else!"

Thursday, September 16, 1897

On the way back from dinner at Marly at Mme B.'s, Joseph Reinach [1] took me aside and said:

"Last June the deputy president of the Senate, Scheurer-Kestner, the former representative of Alsace in the National Assembly, who has had the curiosity to study the Dreyfus case, has come to the conclusion that Dreyfus is innocent, and actually believes that he has discovered the real criminal, another officer. [2] So far Scheurer-Kestner has kept silent, in order to avoid reviving public passions during Félix Faure's journey to Russia, [3] but henceforward nothing will stop him from proclaiming that Dreyfus is the victim of an er-

[1] Joseph Reinach (1856–1921) was a close collaborator of Gambetta's. He was deputy for the Basses-Alpes from 1889 to 1898 and from 1906 to 1914. He was best known as a publicist and was one of the principal artisans of Dreyfus' rehabilitation. His *Histoire de l'affaire Dreyfus* appeared in seven volumes between 1901 and 1911.

[2] Auguste Scheurer-Kestner, an industrialist, born at Mulhouse, Alsace, in 1833, was elected deputy for the Haut-Rhin to the National Assembly in 1871. With all the representatives of Alsace and Lorraine, he protested against its annexation by Germany and resigned after the vote on the peace preliminaries. He was re-elected, became a life senator in 1875, and was a deputy president of the Senate from 1896 onward. He died in 1899.

[3] *Author's note:* Félix Faure left for Russia with Hanotaux on August 18; he returned to Paris on August 31. It was a triumphant journey. In the farewell toasts exchanged between the Czar and the President on board the "Pothuau" the alliance between the two countries was for the first time announced officially; previously only their friendship had been talked of.

ror of justice. He believes that the honor of the Republic requires the reparation of this appalling mistake. Now, I know Scheurer-Kestner well; he is a man
of great courage, stubborn will, and very noble character; I assure you that he will continue to the end
with the generous mission that he has undertaken.''

Then, appealing to our long-standing friendship, he
tried to get me to talk about the 1894 trial.

''All I know about the Dreyfus case I learned in the
course of my duties,'' I told him bluntly. ''I, therefore,
have no right to discuss it with anyone. Nevertheless,
I admit that I am very astonished by what you have
just told me; to my mind, there is no doubt about Dreyfus' guilt.''

''Nevertheless you will permit me one question,''
Reinach persisted. ''No doubt you remember an article
in the *Éclair* just a year ago that disclosed for the first
time that Dreyfus was mentioned by name in an intercepted letter from Schwartzkoppen to Panizzardi. Do
you know that it was the secret submission to the court
of this document that persuaded the court to convict?''

''I know nothing about it.''

Wednesday, November 3, 1897

Leaving the Foreign Ministry at about seven o'clock
this evening, I met Major Henry on the Quai d'Orsay.
He told me that he was going to be promoted to lieutenant-colonel. I congratulated him, and then he started
talking about the campaign to have the case reopened.

As our conversation immediately became very serious, we continued it as we went along on the Esplanade des Invalides.

"I confess," I said to Henry, "that I am very worried by the movement of opinion in favor of reopening the case. It is appearing in the most varied environments. When I see two men as different as Cassagnac and Clemenceau, one an out-and-out Catholic and Monarchist and the other a frantic anti-clerical and Republican, both proclaiming that the mystery that surrounds the conviction of Dreyfus must at all costs be cleared up because we are no longer "in the age of the Man in the Iron Mask," I cannot help feeling acutely anxious. Also, I have had another look at our file on the case. I have just finished re-reading it, document by document, and I have got to the point of wondering whether the 1894 court did not make a mistake."

"Good heavens, no! Reassure yourself on that point," Henry answered in his loud, cheerful voice. "Dreyfus was rightly convicted. Since he has been shark-fishing on his island, we have found the most damning, the most overwhelming, evidence against him. I've got a cupboard full of it!"

"May I know what it consists of?"

"I'll tell you some of it, certainly. But will you give me your word not to repeat it to a soul? It's so serious!"

"Of course! I'll keep your secret for myself alone."

From what he told me, I remember in particular: (1) A letter from Panizzardi to Schwartzkoppen about strategic transport, corresponding both in date and in subject-matter to some work Dreyfus had been ordered to do in 1893; (2) a note from Schwartzkoppen referring to 120 batteries, also corresponding both in date and in subject-matter to work Dreyfus had been ordered to do in 1893; (3) a note from Panizzardi to Schwartzkoppen in which the relations of these two military attachés with Dreyfus are explicitly admitted, Dreyfus' name being actually mentioned.

"Does that satisfy you?" Henry asked.

"I understand less than ever," I said, "because Münster and Tornielli have never ceased assuring Hanotaux that their military attachés never had any dealings whatever with Dreyfus, whether direct or indirect."

Henry made some violent gesticulations in which all his native vulgarity appeared.

"I don't give a damn for what your ambassadors say or don't say," he said. "If they knew about all the documents we found in their embassies, they would stop meddling in the Dreyfus case. We've got something that could give them such a bludgeon stroke that I can guarantee they wouldn't raise their heads again!"

"A bludgeon stroke? You've got something with which you could give them a bludgeon stroke? What do you mean by that?"

"We have an ultra-secret document."

In vain I pressed him to go on, but he was evasive and tried to leave me, so I pointed out that he had told me too much not to tell me everything; I even gave him to understand that if he did not complete his confidences, I would ask General de Boisdeffre to tell me what he had left unsaid.

"General de Boisdeffre!" he exclaimed in alarm, squeezing my arm. "So you want to break me?"

He ended by whispering into my ear:

"We have a letter from the Kaiser."

"A letter from the Kaiser? Addressed to whom?"

"Count von Münster."

"And what does it say?"

"The Kaiser mentions his relations with Dreyfus."

"That's impossible. A sovereign does not correspond with his ambassadors on espionage matters. Are you not confusing it with a letter sent by Münster to Schwartzkoppen from Berlin at the end of January, 1895, which mentions the Kaiser but contains nothing that incriminates Dreyfus?"

"No, it's another, more recent letter, and it does incriminate Dreyfus. But you won't get another word out of me. General Gonse was right to tell me that I ought to be less talkative with you."

And he walked quickly away, with his heavy tread, toward the Invalides.

Saturday, November 6, 1897

Scheurer-Kestner's disclosures are beginning to excite public opinion; the temperature is rising from day to day. The dominant note is surprise, doubt, anxiety. Nobody questions the integrity of the members of the court who pronounced the unanimous verdict of December 22, 1894. Everyone keeps repeating: "Seven officers cannot have agreed to convict an innocent man. Is it likely that all seven could have made a mistake?

And would the War Minister and the General Staff
have set in motion a trial of such gravity in the absence of irrefutable evidence of treason? On the other
hand, Scheurer-Kestner is a serious man, a man of
weight, a patriot, an Alsatian. What has he found
out?''

I was able to judge the extent to which the Dreyfus
case is occupying people's minds when I dined at Mme
Aubernon de Nerville's.[4] Among the guests were Mme
de Pierrebourg, Paul Hervieu, Louis Ganderax, the
philosopher Brochard, the young poet Gregh, etc. They
hoped to get some details from me, but I behaved as
if I knew nothing. So the conversation was confined to
the absurd yarns, the sensational rubbish, with which
the newspapers are filled. Nothing else was talked
about.

Thus for the first time at our hostess' table, there
was talk neither of literature nor of philosophy. A
symptom still more worthy of note was that the conversation did not for one single moment deviate to
love, adultery, or sentimental casuistry.

Lugete veneres cupidinesque!

At the front door Hervieu said to me:

''I do not know what is going to come out of this
affair, but I am certain that I shall see justification,

[4] Euphrasie Héloïse Lydie Lemercier de Nerville (1827–99) was
the wife of Georges Aubernon, who was a Councillor of State. She
separated from him in 1867 and took the name of Aubernon de
Nerville. She had a literary *salon* which was famous in Paris; its
leading spirits were, at first, Alexandre Dumas, *fils*—until 1885—
and, subsequently, Henry Becque, Paul Hervieu, Marcel Prévost,
and Ferdinand Brunetière.

and more than justification, for all that I think of human stupidity and rascality.''

Tuesday, November 16, 1897

The bombshell has burst.

Mathieu Dreyfus, the brother of the convicted man, in a letter to the Minister of War [5] has publicly denounced Count Walsin-Esterhazy, an infantry major, as the author of the *bordereau*, ''the sole basis of the accusation against Captain Dreyfus in 1894.'' He even specified that ''the handwriting of Major Esterhazy is identical with that of the *bordereau*.''

By a strange coincidence Colonel Schwartzkoppen has left suddenly for Berlin, where he is to take command of the 2nd Guard Grenadier Regiment.[6]

In this connection Nisard said to me very knowingly, ''This, if I am not mistaken, is a diplomatic departure. Colonel von Schwartzkoppen evidently prefers

[5] General Billot.

[6] Schwartzkoppen returned to Germany on November 15, 1897. In 1908 he ended a brilliant career there with the rank of general of infantry. In 1914 he volunteered for active service, took part in the operations on the western front until 1915, and in 1916 commanded a division on the Russian front. He died of illness in the Berlin military hospital January 8, 1917. The Dreyfus case haunted him throughout his life; he proclaimed Dreyfus' innocence on his deathbed and in his wife's presence in December, 1916. To justify his conduct in connection with the case, he wrote in 1903 an account that includes the period of which he could speak from his own experience; it stops on November 14, 1896, or a year before his Paris mission came to an end. His widow published it at Hanover in 1930 under the title, *The Truth about Dreyfus*. A French translation appeared the same year in Paris under the title, *Les Carnets de Schwartzkoppen*.

not to be in Paris when Count Walsin-Esterhazy is to
be called to account. Who is this Count Walsin-Esterhazy? Do you know that he is connected with the
famous family of Magyar princes? There was one who
lived through the happy days of Versailles not long
before the Revolution; he even let it be understood that
he had enjoyed the favors of Marie-Antoinette. It certainly would be strange if the traitor of 1894 turned
out to be, not a dirty Jew, but a nobleman of ancient
stock. Since there is a traitor, I'd rather it were an
Esterhazy than a Dreyfus; I should regard it as a
kind of ennoblement for the Republic. But let us be
serious again; for at the bottom of all this, there is an
appalling tragedy and perhaps a great deal of shame
for our country. So you don't know this Walsin-
Esterhazy?"

"No, I have never heard of him."

"Well, then, when you go to the intelligence department try to find out something, but *piano, pianissimo.*"

Wednesday, November 17, 1897

Hanotaux this afternoon received Count von Münster,
who assured him in the most solemn manner: (1) that
Schwartzkoppen had declared to him on his honor that
he had never had any dealings with Captain Dreyfus;
(2) that the *bordereau* had certainly not been found in
the wastepaper of his embassy.

Hanotaux promptly sent me this double-barreled
declaration, with instructions to take it to the General
Staff immediately.

Neither General de Boisdeffre nor General Gonse were in their offices, so I went to see Lieutenant-Colonel Henry to hand it to him.

I found the intelligence department very busy, not to say frantic, because of the investigation of Esterhazy that General de Pellieux, by order of the Governor of Paris, has just opened.

To receive me Henry interrupted a conference with Major Lauth and the archivist Gribelin, both of whom returned a little later to whisper something mysterious in his ear.

I read Münster's statement to Henry, and then showed him a telegram from our chargé d'affaires in Vienna which can be summarized as follows:

Colonel von Schwartzkoppen, talking recently to his friend Prince Lichnowsky, declared to him on his honor that he had never known Captain Dreyfus; the General Staff in Berlin naturally does not know whether Captain Dreyfus had had suspicious relations with the military attaché of any other power.

Henry, who had the peevish and irritable expression of his bad days, replied:

"But we have never maintained that Dreyfus had direct dealings with the German Embassy. Besides, your Vienna representative himself admits the possibility of relations between Dreyfus and the agent of another power. Finally, you know well enough that the intermediary between Dreyfus and Schwartzkoppen was Panizzardi."

"Then how do you explain the telegram of November

2, 1894, in which Panizzardi, spontaneously and at the very first moment, assured the Chief of the Italian General Staff that he had never had any dealings with Dreyfus? You are on the horns of a dilemma. If Dreyfus was in direct contact with the German Embassy, how do you explain Münster's categoric denial? If he was in contact with the Italian Embassy, how do you explain the no less categoric denial in the telegram of November 2, 1894?"

Henry muttered some vague explanations. Then he rose abruptly, opened his safe, and took out a file, which he flung on the table.

"Oh!" he said. "So you want evidence. You shall have it!"

He started reading me a document emanating from Major von Schmettau, the German military attaché in Brussels, when General Gonse came in.

"I was told that you called at my office just now, but I was out with General de Boisdeffre. I came because I thought you might still be here."

I handed him my documents. After he had read them, he turned to Henry, looking uneasy and hesitant, as if he did not know what to say.

Henry, who was standing respectfully between the general and me, resumed his argument.

"When you came in, sir," he said, "I was telling M. Paléologue that these documents prove nothing at all."

"Nothing at all," Gonse repeated after him.

Henry went on firmly:

"We have never maintained that Dreyfus had direct dealings with the German Embassy. Isn't that correct, sir ?"

Gonse, in his hollow voice, muttered between his mustaches:

"We have never maintained that Dreyfus had direct dealings with the German Embassy."

Finally Henry announced:

"The intermediary was Panizzardi."

Gonse echoed in his faltering voice:

"The intermediary was Panizzardi."

I quickly realized that it would be a waste of time to continue the conversation.

"You have given me a great deal to think about," I said to my two interlocutors, and took my leave.

On my way back to the Foreign Ministry through the freezing evening mist, I wondered whether I had not been watching a scene from Shakespeare.

Friday, November 19, 1897

Cavard, the former principal private secretary of the Prefect of Police, who is now in charge of the "external services," that is to say, all the active branches of the Sûreté Générale at the Ministry of the Interior, came to see me to give me certain information about the Russian anarchists who have taken refuge in France. The close watch on these revolutionaries is one of the most delicate and sensitive points, in fact, the "tender spot," of the Franco-Russian alliance.[7]

[7] *Author's note:* The secret aid that the French police gave to the Russian police in the final suppression of nihilism was one of the

We then started talking about the Dreyfus case. Cavard, like me, had been initiated from the beginning, and we had discussed it a number of times.

"Do you know Esterhazy?" I asked him.

"Oh, yes, I know the scoundrel! I've been having him watched by my agents for nearly eight months now."

"Had he been denounced to you?"

"What? So you don't know what has been happening at the intelligence department, or why Picquart has been sent to the depths of Tunisia?"

"No."

---

most decisive factors that led to the Franco-Russian alliance. In May, 1890, when Ribot was Foreign Minister and Constans Minister of the Interior, the police rounded up all the Russian Terrorists who had taken refuge in Paris. Some were extradited, others were expelled, and all their papers were seized and handed over. From that day on nihilism survived only sporadically and harmlessly. To judge the importance of the service rendered to Czardom by the Government of the Republic, it is sufficient to read the following unpublished letter, written by the Baron von Mohrenheim, the Russian Ambassador, on May 29, 1890, in the first flush of his gratitude, to Lozé, the Prefect of Police:

M. LE PRÉFET, *and, let me add, very dear, true, and excellent friend,*

Thank you with all my heart! The signal service that you have just rendered my country is of the kind that can never be esteemed sufficiently highly and can never be forgotten. Terrible misfortunes have been averted thanks to your incomparable energy and the extreme skill of your arrangements. I cannot think without trembling of the disasters that have been spared the Emperor and the whole nation by the sympathetic intervention of the French Government; neither he nor it will ever forget. I myself count for little in such a case; but let me express all the happiness that I personally feel in offering you my heartfelt thanks. I am impatient to shake your hand with all the effusiveness of the most affectionate and unalterable attachment and the most absolute devotion.

(*signed*) MOHRENHEIM.

He then told me that in March Picquart discovered in papers abstracted from the German Embassy a special delivery letter, a *petit bleu,* addressed by Schwartzkoppen to Esterhazy, which for some reason had been torn up instead of being posted. The *petit bleu* made it clear beyond doubt that Esterhazy had had espionage contacts with Schwartzkoppen. The German officer had in fact not written the telegram himself; he had borrowed for the purpose, as he often did, the hand of his delightful little mistress, Mme de Weede, the wife of the Counselor at the Netherlands Legation. Now, the intelligence department had abstracted from Schwartzkoppen's possession sixty letters written by Mme de Weede; the handwriting confirmed the origin of the *petit bleu.* To clear the matter up, Picquart had asked the Sûreté Nationale to have Esterhazy watched, and a police superintendent and a few clever sleuths were put on his heels, with the result that he was seen entering the German Embassy two or three times. As for his private life, the information obtained was appalling. Cavard, whose honest face grew purple with indignation, produced a torrent of derogatory epithets to describe Esterhazy.

"He's an adventurer, a blackguard, a cheat, a swindler, a pimp, a pillar of the brothel and the bawdyhouse, and he sweats vice, wickedness, and treason."

"How heated you're getting! But aren't you rather blackening the man's character? Because what you're saying doesn't fit in at all with the picture of him given me the other day by General Gonse."

"What did Gonse say about him?"

"He said: 'Major Esterhazy is hard up, a spend-thrift, a madcap, a maniac, but he's an honest man, and a fine officer.' " [8]

"So General Gonse has not told you why Picquart is no longer in charge of the intelligence department?"

"Explained, no. All he said was that he had had to get rid of Picquart because he had neither the aptitude nor the mentality for the position." [9]

[8] Charles Walsin-Esterhazy, born in Paris in 1847, was the son of a French general who claimed to be illegitimately connected with the famous Esterházy family of Hungarian princes. Orphaned and ruined at the age of twenty-two, he enlisted in the Papal Zouaves. In June, 1870, he joined the Foreign Legion as a second-lieutenant and fought in the 1870 war. In 1872 he was sent to Africa and subsequently became a lieutenant in the 51st Infantry Regiment. In 1876 he was transferred to the intelligence service, in which he served at the same time as Lieutenant Henry. He was promoted to captain in 1881 and took part in the Tunisian campaign in the following year. In 1892 he was promoted to major, first with the 110th Infantry Regiment at Dunkirk and then with the 74th Regiment at Rouen.

[9] In July, 1895, General de Boisdeffre had forbidden Lieutenant-Colonel Picquart, the new chief of the intelligence department, to pursue inquiries into the Dreyfus case and, in particular, to inquire into what might have been the motive for the crime for which Dreyfus had been sentenced. Picquart had gradually become convinced of Dreyfus' innocence while at the same time his suspicions of Major Esterhazy had been roused. Picquart became suspect to his chiefs, particularly General Gonse, and was removed from the intelligence department on the pretext of being sent on a mission to the east; he was assigned to the 4th Tirailleurs and sent to southern Tunisia. He was recalled to Paris in November, 1897, was court-martialed in January, 1898, and on February 26, 1898, was cashiered for "grave service misdemeanors."

Lieutenant-Colonel Picquart was reinstated and promoted to brigadier-general by the law of July 13, 1906. He died a lieutenant-general on January 18, 1914.

I did not press the matter but asked Cavard how it was possible for an officer with a character as badly stained as Esterhazy's not to have been thrown out of the army long ago.

"Because he enjoys some very high and very powerful patronage in the army; he is an intimate friend of Maurice Weil. Do you understand now?"

"I fear I understand only too well."

Saturday, November 20, 1897

Our great detective Cavard told me yesterday that Esterhazy was an intimate friend of Weil.

Now, here is the improbable story of this Jew.

Maurice Weil was born in 1844 and served in 1870–71 in the Army of the Loire as an officer of the militia; General Berthaut had attached him to his staff. He distinguished himself sufficiently to be awarded the Legion of Honor at the end of the war.

In 1875, thanks to the influence of General de Cissey —who was to be ruined a few years later in the shameful adventure of the Baronne de Kaulla—he secured a post as a captain of the reserve to the intelligence department, which was then in charge of Colonel Samuel; Henry, then a young lieutenant, had just been given a place in the same department by General de Miribel.

In his private life, Maurice Weil divided his time between historical studies and speculations on the Bourse, bringing tireless energy and a penetrating mind to bear on both. In addition to this, he had plenty of assurance and address and a great deal of amiability; he is a brilliant talker and much appreciated by women. In 1876, he married an elegant Viennese, a co-religionist.

At the same time General Berthaut, his wartime chief, became Minister of War. Weil had himself attached to his private office, where he dealt with press relations. He took advantage of this to establish relations with the big men of the period, Generals Lewal, Saussier, Warnet, etc. His studies of the wars of the First Empire gave him an excuse for continually consulting them on strategic questions.

Simultaneously he frequented the *salons* of Jewish high finance and was an assiduous visitor at the Rothschilds, the Ephrussys, the Cahen d'Anvers, the Camondos; he was even said to be the lover of a beautiful Jewish countess, the wife of a Jewish banker.

He also conceived a passion for horse-racing. He was regularly to be seen in the paddock at Longchamp, Auteuil, and Deauville. He was noticed among the big bettors, but nobody worried, because, on the one hand, he seemed to be possessed of a certain fortune and, on the other, he was known often to lay bets on behalf of his wealthy friends.

But disaster came one fine day at Deauville in the summer of 1881. The Baron de Schikler discovered that Weil, who was acting for him, had cheated him. Weil was denounced by the *Vie moderne.*

The public scandal forced him to resign from the army reserve. He was summoned to appear before a court of inquiry, but fled to Spain, where he remained for some months.

The brilliant situation which he had built up for himself in Paris was in ruins. But with that mixture of flexibility and tenacity that is one of the marks of his race, he set about gradually re-establishing it.

By a stroke of brilliant cynicism, he secured the friendship of the Commander-in-Chief, the Governor of Paris, General Saussier who, having a lively sensual appetite in spite of his sixty years, became the lover of the attractive Mme Weil.

Thus, on January 8, 1890, the complaisant husband was restored to the army with the rank of major of territorial cavalry and assigned to the Commander-in-Chief's staff.

Henceforward, he was his chief's inseparable companion; General Saussier dined with his good friends two or three times a week.

This intimacy with the Commander-in-Chief naturally procured the Weil couple innumerable invitations and favors in the military world.

However, the most insulting rumors began to circulate about them; they were suspected of espionage on behalf of Germany, using Austria as a go-between.

In May, 1892, an article in the *Libre Parole,* over the signature of the Marquis de Morès, actually said: "In the Military Government of Paris there is an all-powerful Jewish swindler named Weil, who does all its dirty work. This man, known to all sportsmen as a thief, has his big and little entrées into the national defense."

On reading this article the Commander-in-Chief shrugged his shoulders, and Weil smiled.

Morès continued his campaign in the press and at
public lectures. The Commander-in-Chief continued to
shrug his shoulders, and Weil continued to smile.

Casimir-Perier, who was on very friendly terms
with General Saussier, tried to open his eyes, but in
vain.

"You don't imagine that I am going to allow myself
to be influenced by the twaddle in the *Libre Parole!*"
was the single argument behind which he retreated.

However, in February, 1893, Morès's attacks became so violent and Casimir-Perier's representations
so pressing that the Commander-in-Chief at last admitted the moral impossibility of retaining Weil on
his staff—which did not prevent him from remaining
the intimate of the Jewish couple.

In December, 1894, the doubts about Dreyfus' guilt
which General Saussier did not hesitate to express
were attributed to Weil's influence.[10]

Tuesday, November 23, 1897

One of our secret informers, the Baron de Saint-
Aubanet, a former naval officer, called on me this morning in the Boulevard Malesherbes to give me an ac-

[10] Maurice Weil was born in Paris in 1845. In 1870 he was a lieutenant in the militia and served in the war as General Berthaut's
aide-de-camp. When the latter became War Minister in 1876, he appointed Weil to his staff with the rank of captain of territorial
infantry. He was relieved of his duties on the War Minister's staff
on April 13, 1880, and assigned to the staff of the territorial army
on February 7, 1890. On June 4, 1892, he was appointed to the staff
of General Saussier, the Military Governor of Paris, and resigned
on April 26, 1893. He died in 1924.

count of a very delicate mission which he has just completed in Italy.

He is a most original character. He is sixty-five years old, very alert, spick and span, very well-dressed, always has a flower in his buttonhole, has been very fond of women and is still able to please them, and adores intrigue, adventure, and nosing about. In 1891 he was pointed out, or rather handed over, to us by the Prefect of Police, Lozé, who recognized his astonishing skill in worming his way into the most varied environments and eliciting information; for the rest, he is a decent enough chap. Nisard and I always refer to him as "Casanova" or "M. de Seingalt." He was in good form today because he had had good hunting in a certain Roman *palazzo*.

Before he left I asked him whether in the course of his stormy life he had ever met Esterhazy.

"It would be too much to say that I ever knew him," he replied, "but I used to meet him sometimes, particularly eighteen or twenty years ago, when he worked for the intelligence service. He has a face you can't forget. I recognized him immediately the other evening at *Figaro*. He has fiery eyes, a sallow complexion, a contracted mouth, and a vulture's head; added to that, he has a nerve and a self-assurance of which I've never seen the like; he's a mixture of bully and *condottiere*. At the time I was telling you about he reigned over the heart (I am being polite) of Léonide Leblanc— you know, the beautiful actress of the Comédie française who was the mistress of the Duc d'Aumale—she

of course also slept with Monseigneur's aide-de-camp,
young Captain Berthaut, the son of the Minister of
War.''

"That's very interesting. But tell me, was not Ester-
hazy at that time on terms of close friendship with a
Jew whom there's some talk about these days, one
Maurice Weil?''

"I couldn't tell you; I don't know anything about
Maurice Weil.''

At the Ministry I told Nisard what "Casanova'' had
said and went on:

"Think what the association of these two men, Esterhazy and Weil, may have been about the year 1878.
One was the favorite lover of a courtesan who shared
her favors between a lieutenant-general and the son
of the Minister of War; the other procured his wife
for the Commander-in-Chief.''

"Did not 'M. de Seingalt' also tell you that at the
same period Lieutenant Henry was spending his novi-
tiate in the intelligence service?''

Nisard fell silent and looked at me with his sharp,
searching eyes. Then, in a slow, precise voice, as if
weighing every word, he said:

"Perhaps we now have the leading thread in our
hands—the thread of Ariadne. But what shall we find
in the labyrinth?''

Monday, November 29, 1897

I went to see General de Boisdeffre and handed him:

(1) A statement by Count von Münster to Hanotaux saying: "I have always believed in Dreyfus' innocence, and my Embassy has never had the slightest contact with that officer." This statement was made on November 24 in confirmation of the statement made on November 17.

(2) A statement by Count Tornielli to Hanotaux saying: "Colonel Panizzardi finds himself obliged to make a public announcement denying that he ever wrote the phrases alleged to have been written by him referring to Dreyfus, whether by name, initial, or any other designation. Further, he asks to be allowed to state this under oath in court." This statement was made on November 27, the day before yesterday.

(3) A summary of telegrams exchanged between the Italian Ambassador in Paris and the Marchese Visconti-Venosta, the Foreign Minister in Rome. These telegrams were in the Embassy's most confidential code, but our deciphering service succeeded in breaking it down. The telegrams, dated November 21 and 23, leave no doubt about the sincerity of the statement above.

General de Boisdeffre carefully read the three documents. Then, in his tired, bored voice, he said to me:
"Will you leave me these papers?"
"Yes, I am delivering them to you officially. Also I know that M. Hanotaux talked about them to General Billot [11] this morning."

[11] Jean-Baptiste Billot (1828–1907) took part in the Algerian and Mexican campaigns. In 1870 he was the Chief of Staff of a division

"I shall talk to him about them this evening."

He put the papers on his desk with an indifferent gesture and, as if to change the subject, went on:

"Ah! my dear Paléologue, what an odious business! We two at any rate have something more interesting to talk about. Have you any news from Russia?"

The conversation was immediately diverted to foreign affairs and to the changes in the European balance that would inevitably follow the official announcement of the Franco-Russian alliance.

From Boisdeffre's office, I went down to the intelligence department, where I informed Lieutenant-Colonel Henry of the statements made by Münster and Tornielli.

After the first few words Henry interrupted me in a surly voice, with an ugly expression on his face, and a hard and mistrustful look in his eyes.

"Your ambassadors are brazen liars!" he said. "After all that I've told you and all that I've shown you, how is it that you don't see that they're trying to pull wool over your eyes?"

in the fighting around Metz. On the surrender of Metz he escaped and went to Tours, where Gambetta had him promoted to colonel and subsequently brigadier-general. He was elected a deputy to the National Assembly, sat with the Republican Left, and took an active part in military debates. He was War Minister in the Freycinet and Duclerc Cabinets from January 30, 1882, to January 31, 1883, and resigned in protest against the law forbidding the Princes of Orléans to serve in the army. He again became Minister of War in the Méline Cabinet in April, 1896. He remained convinced of Dreyfus' guilt in spite of the efforts of his close friend Scheurer-Kestner and never ceased to oppose the reopening of the case.

"But Tornielli's and Visconti-Venosta's deciphered telegrams put the sincerity of their statements beyond dispute."

"And what do you make of Dreyfus' confession?"

"Dreyfus confessed? When did he do that?"

Henry told me that on the morning of the degradation Dreyfus said in conversation with Captain Lebrun-Renaud, who was his escort until the time of the parade: "The Minister knows very well that if I delivered documents to Germany, it was in order to obtain more important documents in return."

"And this confession was officially recorded?"

"Certainly!"

"Then the mystery of 1894 is even deeper than I thought."

Tuesday, November 30, 1897

I went to see Casimir-Perier and told him my doubts about Dreyfus' guilt.

"You don't surprise me," he said. "I'm beginning to be shaken myself."

I told him all that I had recently found out, and we compared our memories. We looked at each other with growing anxiety. Suddenly the same idea struck both of us.

"It would be terrible!" exclaimed Casimir-Perier, whose face had suddenly become bloodless and ashen—a symptom I have too often noticed in him; it seems to indicate some sort of heart trouble.

Then, reverting to my former certainty, I said:

"All the same, there are the convicted man's confessions."

"What confessions?"

"Those that Captain Lebrun-Renaud came and told you about at the Élysée on the day after the degradation." [12]

"Captain Lebrun-Renaud told me nothing about any confession. What is this new story?"

I told him what Lieutenant-Colonel Henry told me yesterday in such detail.

"He lied!" Casimir-Perier exclaimed. "I remember very well that on the day after the degradation, that is to say on January 6, 1895, the War Minister sent Captain Lebrun-Renaud of the Republic Guard to me, to tell me what Dreyfus said on the way from the Cherche-Midi prison to the École militaire. General Mercier incidentally asked me to give that officer a good dressing-down because the evening before, at a Montmartre café, he had told some journalists that the principal document in the case had been found in the German Embassy, which might have made difficulties in the con-

---

[12] One of the subjects of most heated controversy in the Dreyfus case was the confession said to have been made by Dreyfus on the morning of his degradation to Captain of Gendarmerie Lebrun-Renaud, who escorted him to the École militaire. Now, none of the official reports written after the degradation ceremony (including that of Captain Lebrun-Renaud himself) refers to any confession, the absence of which was officially put forward by the War Ministry as a reason for subjecting Dreyfus to a particularly rigorous form of imprisonment. Nevertheless, Captain Lebrun-Renaud in October, 1897, wrote out and signed a document declaring that the confession had been made. True, he did so on the demand and in the presence of General Gonse.

versation I was going to have with Münster. I received
Lebrun-Renaud at about ten o'clock in the morning, if
I am not mistaken. He had nothing interesting to say
whatever. I gave him a good talking to for wagging his
tongue at Montmartre, he muttered some excuses, and
that was all. As for any confession by Dreyfus, he said
nothing whatever about it; otherwise you can be sure
that I should have made him dictate it to me because
of the excellent use I should have been able to make of
it in my conversation with Münster."

After a long, overwhelming silence, he went on:

"All this, my dear friend, portends a terrible scandal
for our army. Heaven preserve us from going as far as
civil war!"

Wednesday, December 1, 1897

For some days past, there has been a flood of disclosures in the press. *Figaro,* in particular, has been
publishing a series of letters written by Esterhazy to
a former mistress, Mme de Boulancy, the widow of a
colonel. They were written in 1882, during the Tunisian
campaign, are dated from Sousse, Kairouan, and Sfax,
and are nothing but a long diatribe, an interminable
litany of invective, insult, sarcasm, execration, blas-
phemy, and threats against France. In the whole literature of pamphleteering, I know of nothing more violent, more pungent, or more poisonous; spite and malice
have perhaps never been more vigorously expressed.
Moreover, as it is passion that makes style, these epis-

tles are admirable in color and embellishment, violence
and crudity. I note at random a few passages only:

*Great events are in preparation, and in the first real
war all our great leaders, who are ignoramuses and
cowards, will be ridiculously beaten and will once more
populate the German prisons, which will be too small
to contain them. . . . Before long the Germans will put
all these people in their real place. . . . Such is the fine
army of France. And but for the question of my position, I should leave tomorrow. I have written to Constantinople. If they offer me a rank that suits me, I
shall go there; but I shall not leave without having
played a joke of my own kind on these scum. . . . All
our French generals still have the mark of the Prussian boot in a place lower than their backs; they tremble with fear at their own shadow. . . . I am absolutely
convinced that killing these people is not worth the
expenditure of a bullet. . . . If I were told this evening
that I were to die tomorrow as a captain of uhlans
sabering Frenchmen, I should be perfectly happy. . . .
Ah! why cannot I see Paris, under a red sun of battle,
taken by assault and handed over to be looted by a
hundred thousand drunken soldiers?*

These letters, which it is impossible to read in cold
blood, which set one's brain on fire, make Esterhazy
appear, not just a crude old soldier, but a high-grade
buccaneer, a rogue in the grand style. To describe such
a man, no less than a Balzac or a Saint-Simon would
be needed.

Figaro, not content with publishing these letters, also publishes a photograph of the original, together with a facsimile of the *bordereau,* thus making it possible to compare the handwriting of Dreyfus with that of Esterhazy. So far as one can judge without having the original before one's eyes, the comparison is damning for the "captain of uhlans."

This afternoon Lieutenant-Colonel Henry came to see me to draw the monthly allocation from secret funds that the Foreign Ministry pays the intelligence service as its contribution to counter-espionage expenditure. No sooner had Henry pocketed the money than he said:

"I am terribly busy today. We're being worked to death over this inquiry of General de Pellieux's."

"But you can't go until you have told me what you think of the letters to Mme de Boulancy."

"That material in the *Figaro* is a disgrace. Those letters are forged, made up of bits and pieces. Major Esterhazy disowns them completely, and General de Pellieux has ordered an expert's report. Believe me, the Dreyfusards won't have the last laugh!"

He made as if to go, but I stopped him at the door.

"Don't you think," I said, "that Esterhazy's handwriting is terribly like that of the *bordereau?*"

"Yes, it is rather like it. But is there anything surprising in that if, as I believe, Dreyfus traced Esterhazy's handwriting to write his *bordereau?* Just wait for the expert opinion. Just wait!"

He left me barely time to shake his hand.

Saturday, December 4, 1897

General Saussier, the Governor of Paris, has ordered an investigation of Major Esterhazy.

Esterhazy himself asked to be brought to trial.

"Having been publicly accused of high treason," he declared, "I have the right to a court-martial, which is the highest form of military justice. Only a decision emanating from the latter will be able to stigmatize the most cowardly of slanderers by my acquittal."

This statement, posted since early morning in the lobbies of the Chamber, caused a sensation.

Two interpellations were immediately tabled, one by Marcel Sembat, the Socialist, and the other by Count Albert de Mun, the Monarchist.

As soon as the House sat Méline,[13] the Prime Minister, announced: "I shall say right away what will be the decisive word in this debate: There is no Dreyfus case."

Lively applause from all benches, except the extreme Left. Méline evidently meant to say that there was no connection between the conviction of Dreyfus and the proceedings against Esterhazy, for the Dreyfus case was closed.

Albert de Mun then went to the rostrum and with an imperious gesture put a light to the powder barrel.

[13] Jules Méline (1838–1925), became a deputy for the Vosges in 1872, was Minister of Agriculture from 1883 to 1885 and Prime Minister and Minister of Agriculture from April 30, 1896, to June 30, 1898.

Assuming the role of defender of the country and of the army, he denounced the Jewish syndicate which had put itself in German pay. "It must be known," he declared in his fine, sonorous voice, "it must be known whether it is true that there is in this country a mysterious, occult power strong enough to be able, at its pleasure, to throw suspicion on the leaders of our army, on those whose task it will be, on the day when great duties devolve upon them, to lead our army against the enemy and conduct war. It must be known whether this occult power is really strong enough to throw the whole country into the confusion that has existed for more than a fortnight. . . . Ah! Mr. Prime Minister, you asked that politics should not enter into this. No, there is no question of politics here. Here there are neither friends nor opponents of the Cabinet: there are only Frenchmen, anxious to preserve intact their most precious possession, that which remains in the midst of our struggles and our discords, the common domain of our invincible hopes: the honor of the army!"

Nearly the whole Chamber rose to acclaim this magnificent language.

General Billot, the War Minister, mounted the rostrum and said in his turn:

"The Dreyfus case was justly and regularly tried. As for myself, I solemnly and sincerely declare, as a soldier and leader of the army, that I believe Dreyfus to be guilty."

There was frantic applause.

In the evening I met Eugène Melchior de Vogüé at

Mme B.'s, who is one of our common friends. He was still full of the day's events in Parliament.

"Albert de Mun surpassed himself," he said to us. "He roused the whole Chamber. He was as admirable to watch as to listen to; his proud attitude, his supple gestures, his warm, pungent, imperious voice, the purity of his style, the breadth of his rhythmic phrases. . . . Oh! what a fine portrait Cormenin would have made of him!"

"Do his portrait yourself. You're as good as Cormenin!"

Monday, December 13, 1897

Dined at Henri Germain's,[14] the chairman of the Crédit Lyonnais. There were present the sculptor Guillaume, the director of the Villa Médicis, Eugène Melchior de Vogüé, and my old friend from the Lycée Louis-le-Grand, Raymond Poincaré.[15]

We talked of nothing but the Dreyfus case.

Poincaré, who was Finance Minister in 1894 and was present at the famous meeting of Ministers held on November 1, maintained great reserve, even toward me. He confined himself to saying:

"It is essentially a judicial matter. It should be left

[14] Henri Germain (1824–1905) was the founder of the Crédit Lyonnais and was its chairman until his death. He was a member of the Chamber of Deputies in 1869 and again from 1871 to 1886 and from 1889 to 1893 and regularly took part in financial debates.

[15] Raymond Poincaré, deputy for the Meuse since 1887, had been Education Minister in the Casimir-Perier Cabinet (April-December, 1893) and Finance Minister in the second Dupuy Cabinet (May, 1894-January, 1895).

to the courts and not dragged about in the marketplace, as is happening now.''

Vogüé attributed the role being played by Zola to his extraordinary self-conceit.

''Voltaire,'' he said, ''the prince of eighteenth-century men of letters, went to the defense of Calas; the prince of nineteenth-century literary men, Zola, has to be the apologist for Dreyfus.'' [16]

Everyone agreed in foreseeing a violent recrudescence of anti-Semitism in France, and subsequently of anti-Protestantism.

Vogüé also said:

''I have just been re-reading the Book of Esther. It made me understand the solidarity that the Jews are now showing and the passionate ardor with which all of them, without distinction of rank, are trying to obtain reparation for a wrong done to one of them.''

''So,'' I said, ''you think that an Esther is engaged in steeping herself in myrrh and spices, waiting for President Faure to open his bed to her?''

''You're still the same!'' Poincaré said to me.

Guillaume told us of a saying of Paul Bourget's, who is nowadays ferociously anti-Semitic, though he used to be a frequent visitor at Jewish *salons*. ''I hate Jews because they crucified Jesus,'' he said. ''I adore Jewesses because they wept for Him.''

Henri Germain, who is a stickler for exactness and is always inquisitive about figures, asked:

''Is it known more or less how many Jews there are in France and in the world?''

[16] Zola was to publish *J'Accuse,* his open letter to the President of the Republic, in the *Aurore* on January 13 in the following year.

"I think I can tell you," I said, "because I recently made inquiries of a good source. The total number of Jews in the world is approximately twelve million, of whom there are five million in Russia, two million in Austria, 600,000 in Germany, and 180,000 in the United States. In France there are not more than 80,000, of whom 42,000 live in Paris."

Germain made a rapid calculation.

"The population of France being thirty-nine million, that makes about one Jew to every five hundred Frenchmen."

"There's certainly nothing to worry us about those proportions," Vogüé went on. "But I should like to know how many of those 80,000 Jews occupy public offices. That is the percentage that worries me."

Tuesday, December 21, 1897

While the judge-advocate of the Army Council is preparing the Esterhazy case, and consequently the Dreyfus case is in the doldrums, the trial of Arton and the parliamentarians compromised in the Panama scandal is taking place in the Assize Court. The interval has thus been filled. It is as if a skillful impresario were organizing and timing scandals so as to insure that the stage is never empty.

Thursday, December 30, 1897

The Panama trial ended today in the Assize Court.

There was a general acquittal all round. Thus the last shovelful of earth flung on the year 1897 has been a shovelful of mud.

3. STEPS TO RETRIAL

3 . STEPS TO
RETRIAL

Sunday, January 2, 1898

General Saussier, considering that the inquiries into the case of Major Esterhazy "have not produced sufficient light," has ordered him to be court-martialed.

Drumont and Rochefort claim that this eminently reasonable decision is a "victory for the Jewish syndicate."

Saussier, having reached the age limit, is to be put on the retired list in a few days' time.

Tuesday, January 11, 1898

Esterhazy appeared today and yesterday before a court-martial presided over by General de Luxer. The court sat twice daily, nearly the whole time *in camera*.

After five minutes' deliberation, it returned a unanimous verdict of not guilty.

As soon as he appeared at the prison gateway Esterhazy was acclaimed by a delirious mob, yelling:

"Long live the army! Long live Esterhazy! Death to the Jews!"

Saturday, January 15, 1898

I spent a long time with Lieutenant-Colonel Henry, who described the Esterhazy trial to me.

"General de Luxer presided superbly," he said. "I assure you that the Dreyfusard witnesses—Scheurer-Kestner, Mathieu Dreyfus, and company—didn't pipe up. As for Picquart, he was crushed; he is going to be referred to a court of inquiry to explain his machinations."

Henry, with an admirable unawareness, congratulated himself highly on the role played behind the scenes by General de Pellieux.[1]

"In the main," he went on, "it was Pellieux who conducted the proceedings. He sat behind the presiding officer's chair and whispered to him every now and then. Pellieux is a fine soldier, you know, a very fine soldier. While he was investigating Esterhazy, I confidentially showed him Panizzardi's letter to Schwartz-

[1] General de Pellieux, as General Officer Commanding the Seine Department, had been ordered by General Saussier, acting on the instructions of General Billot, the Minister of War, to undertake an inquiry about Major Esterhazy. In his report, submitted in November, 1897, General Pellieux exonerated Esterhazy and accused Lieutenant-Colonel Picquart of grave dereliction of duty.

koppen in which Dreyfus' name is mentioned. He was stunned, dumfounded; he couldn't believe his eyes!"

I interrupted him.

"Could I not see that letter?" I asked. "You are always talking about it, but you never show it to me."

"I can't show it to you; it's not in my possession any longer. General Gonse has it in a sealed envelope in his safe."

"Supposing I asked General Gonse to show it to me?"

"He won't; he's holding it in reserve for great occasions. But as I've told you what it contains, why do you want so much to see it?"

"Because it interests me greatly."

He did not pursue the matter, but rose, went over to his safe, took a document from it, and passed it to me.

"Read that!" he said. "It's a note from the Austrian military attaché, Colonel Schneider. We received it on November 30 last; you'll see that Schneider firmly believes in Dreyfus' guilt."

Henry authorized me to take a copy of the note for our files. It was as follows:

It has often been suggested that the traitor is someone other than Dreyfus, and I should not have returned to the matter if for the past year my German and Italian colleagues had not been maintaining this in the salons. . . . As for myself, I still believe that Dreyfus was in contact with the Brussels and Strasbourg espionage services.

"Well!" Henry said to me. "That's clear enough, isn't it?"

"At any rate it's very curious."

This evening I dined at Mme Aubernon's. There were present the Baronne de Pierrebourg, Paul Hervieu, Brunetière, Larroumet,[2] René Bazin, Brochard,[3] and Séailles.[4]

Hervieu, Larroumet, Brochard and Séailles are ardent advocates of a retrial; Bazin and Brunetière are in the opposite camp.

The discussion immediately assumed an impassioned note. Brunetière was not satisfied with defending his views: he attracted all the blows to himself; he even provoked them, for the sake of the sharp pleasure of returning them.

I note at random a few of his statements or replies:

"Without courts, there can be no society, gentlemen! Therefore have respect for the *res judicata*. Do not destroy institutions that you yourselves set up. . . . You tell me the Republic resents seeing all the old parties banding together against it. But whose fault is it but her own? Why for the last twenty years has it

[2] Gustave Larroumet (1852–1903) had been Professor of French Literature at the Sorbonne and in 1888 director of the Beaux Arts. He was elected a member of the Académie des Beaux Arts in 1891 and its perpetual secretary in 1898.

[3] Victor Brochard (1848–1907) had succeeded Emile Boutroux as lecturer in philosophy at the École Normale Supérieure and in 1894 had become Professor of Ancient Philosophy at the Sorbonne.

[4] Gabriel Séailles (1852–1922) was a lecturer and, subsequently, a professor of philosophy at the Sorbonne.

banished from the political arena all those who had
previously distinguished themselves in the Chambers,
in the administration, in diplomacy? Why has it ostra-
cized all the representatives of the old French traditions? Why have Protestants, free-thinkers, Freemasons, Jews, got hold of all the public offices? . . .
And what is M. Zola up to? His letter, *J'Accuse*, is a
monument of stupidity, presumptuousness, and ab-
surdity. This novelist's meddling in a problem of military justice seems to me no less impertinent and
preposterous than the intervention of a captain of
gendarmerie in a question of syntax or prosody. . . .

"And this petition which is being circulated among
the 'intellectuals.' The sole fact that the word 'intellectual' has recently been coined for the purpose of
setting apart in a kind of exalted social category people who spend their lives in laboratories and libraries
points to one of the most absurd eccentricities of our
time, namely, the claim that writers, scientists, professors, philologists should be elevated to the rank of
supermen. I certainly do not despise intellectual abil-
ities, but their value is only relative. I place will power,
force of character, sureness of judgment, practical experience, higher in the social scale. I know farmers and
merchants whom I do not hesitate to place far above
certain scholars, biologists, and mathematicians whose
names I do not care to mention."

Paul Hervieu, Séailles, Larroumet, and Brochard
were not slow to reply: "Certainly justice is the foundation of society, but justice is based, not on law courts,
but on law. . . . A man's honor is no less precious than

the honor of an army.... The idea of an innocent man's being convicted is intolerable to anyone with even a spark of pity in his heart.... Remember the admirable phrase of Cicero's: 'Justice is nothing other than love of the human race': *'Ipsa caritas generis humani'*.... To convict a man on charges of which he is unaware is not only an illegality, but also a judicial murder. Reasons of state are most often only a convenient mantle to cover the ignorance, stupidity, or wickedness of an oligarchy.... It is not the generals or Rochefort, or Cavaignac, or the brawlers of the *Libre Parole,* or the protectors of Esterhazy, or even your Duc d'Orléans, who today represent the true traditions of the French mind and the French conscience, but the intellectuals.''

Walking home, I thought that in spite of all the violence and invective, all the scandals, and all the abuse by which France is rent, the drama is not lacking in grandeur, since it has set at grips two sacred feelings, love of justice and patriotism.

Tuesday, January 18, 1898

General Billot, acting in the name of the court-martial that has just acquitted Esterhazy, has lodged with the Seine court notice of an action for libel against Zola and the manager of the *Aurore.* The case is expected to be heard in the Assize Court early in February.

This evening I went to the Schérer dinner (the former Magny dinner) at the Foyot restaurant. Among those present were Émile Gebhart, Michel Bréal, Salomon Reinach, Anatole Leroy-Beaulieu, D'Eichtal, Raphaël Georges-Lévy, Pierre Janet, Lévy-Bruhl, etc.

Toward the end of dinner conversation turned to the Dreyfus case. I was put under cross-examination from nine to eleven o'clock and had great difficulty in reconciling my private opinion, that is to say my growing doubts, with my official position. When I saw Hanotaux this morning and told him how I expected to spend the evening, he could not repress an outburst of petulance. "Oh! be on your guard against those people!" he exclaimed. "These intellectuals, who used to be my colleagues, my friends, I might almost say my coreligionists, have become detestable to me. The campaign they are conducting against the Government, and above all against me, is abominable. Beware of them! You can be sure that, however little you tell them, they will publish, exaggerate, and distort what you say. Be on your guard!"

I watched my tongue all the more carefully because the conversation from the outset became lively and heated, though on a very high plane; I imagine that at the beginning of the Wars of Religion, at the time of the Chambre Ardente, about 1547, similar conversations were being held throughout French society.

This, then, was more or less what I said: "The Dreyfus case is very obscure and very complicated; the very nature of the evidence, whether for or against the convicted man, makes it a very delicate matter, because most of it cannot be produced in the light of day, for its source cannot be admitted. It is in fact impossible to bring the whole organization of our espionage and counter-espionage services into the forum of public debate. Think of the repercussions there would be in the diplomatic field!''

Salomon Reinach [5] challanged this statement with asperity.

"We already know that argument," he said. "It sums up the whole policy of your Minister who, I have no need to tell you, has forfeited our friendship and esteem. But here is a question I put to you, to you personally, addressed to your own conscience. Do you believe that a public trial of the Dreyfus case, a trial in which all the documents, all the evidence, were publicly exhibited in court—do you believe that such a trial might lead to war?''

"War? I do not know because when public passions are once roused no one can tell where they will stop. However, I admit that in the present European situation, there would not be an immediate danger of war. But I am certain that if we allowed the whole mechanism of our secret services to be discussed in a public court, we should expose ourselves to grave diplomatic complications. Indeed, Germany could not ask for a better opportunity of inflicting a national humiliation on us. Look at the picture we are offering the world: every French family divided, the leaders of our army suspect or the subject of aspersion, every department of government thrown out of gear, the whole of European opinion roused against us! Even Russia seems to mistrust us, since she has just changed her War

[5] Salomon Reinach (1858–1932), the well-known ancient historian and archaeologist, the director of the Museum of National Antiquities at St. Germain, was the brother of Joseph Reinach.

Minister, General Vanovski, and her Chief of Staff,
General Obruchev, who were the warmest partisans of
the French alliance.''

I concluded: ''So long as calm is not re-established
in people's minds, so long as the Dreyfus case remains
on the passionate and mystic level, the puzzle of 1894
will remain insoluble.''

These words seemed to make a pretty deep impression on those listening to me.

Tuesday, January 25, 1898

Yesterday, while Méline, the Prime Minister, in reply
to an interpellation by Cavaignac and remonstrances
by Jaurès, was once more proclaiming in the Chamber
that Dreyfus was guilty, Count von Bülow,[6] Secretary
of State in the German Foreign Ministry, was saying
to a committee of the Reichstag:

''I declare in the most formal fashion that there
have never been any relations whatever between the
former Captain Dreyfus, now detained at Devil's Island, and any German agent.''

Thursday, January 27, 1898

This morning, while the Council of Ministers was
meeting at the Ministry of Agriculture (where the
Prime Minister still has his office), I took Hanotaux

[6] Count Bernard von Bülow, who was made Prince von Bülow in
1905, was born in 1849, and entered the diplomatic service in 1874.
He was appointed German Minister to Bucharest (1888) and was
Ambassador to Rome from 1893 to 1897. He became Secretary of
State in the Foreign Ministry in 1897, and was Imperial Chancellor
from 1900 to 1909.

an urgent telegram that he was waiting for impatiently
and had ordered to be brought to him immediately.

He came out of the room in which the meeting was
being held, read the telegram, and made me sit down
near him.

"Let us talk for a bit," he said. "What they are
discussing on the other side of the door is boring, and
I'm glad of a chance of escape. . . . Come, my dear fellow, entirely between ourselves and quite apart from
all official relationships, what do you think of the Dreyfus case, and what do you know about it? I shall not
conceal from you that I am completely baffled."

I told him all that was in my mind on the subject, my
growing doubts, the flagrant contradictions that I
noted between our information and that of the General
Staff. "Take the *bordereau*, for instance, which was
the basis of the 1894 trial. How did it reach the War
Ministry? Colonel Sandherr and Lieutenant-Colonel
Henry have always assured me that it got there by the
'ordinary route,' that is to say through a servant who
ransacked the wastepaper baskets at the German Embassy where she was employed. Well, I no longer believe it. I am convinced that Schwartzkoppen never received the *bordereau* and never had had dealings with
Dreyfus. On the other hand, you remember the telegram Panizzardi sent to the Italian Chief of Staff
immediately after Dreyfus' arrest. That telegram and
the documents that reached us subsequently show beyond any possibility of doubt that Panizzardi never
had dealings with Dreyfus either."

"It is true that Münster and Tornielli have never

ceased to assure me that their military attachés learned the name of Dreyfus only after his arrest. As for the finding of the *bordereau* at the German Embassy, I am afraid you are right. Only the other day, Münster again assured me on his honor that the *bordereau* had not been found in the wastepaper baskets of his Embassy, and that the Germans were in no way involved in the business.''

''And doesn't Schwartzkoppen's sudden departure seem very significant to you? On November 15 Mathieu Dreyfus denounces Esterhazy, and on the same day, with no plausible excuse and without explanation, Schwartzkoppen has himself recalled to Berlin. As soon as he has gone, Münster comes and tells us once more that his military attaché has never had any dealings with Dreyfus. But he takes care not to cover Esterhazy.''

''All that is certainly very remarkable. . . . But you did not make all these striking deductions out of the blue, without thinking them over and checking them. You must have talked to Lieutenant-Colonel Henry about them. What did he say?''

''His answer has always been the same. 'Your ambassadors lie,' he says. 'Since Dreyfus has been at Devil's Island we have found the most overwhelming and unanswerable evidence against him; I've a whole cupboardful, etc.' I do not dare push him too far on that delicate ground because you advised me to be extremely cautious in my relations with the intelligence service.''

''I advise you to be more cautious than ever, my

dear fellow. You know my position; it has not changed since 1894. I consider that the Dreyfus case is exclusively the business of the military judicial authorities, and that our diplomacy has no right to interfere. I consider that my responsibilities in the matter are confined to passing on to the War Ministry the information that comes to my attention, and I shall not be dragged any farther. I know that in acting in this way I expose myself to the fury of the intellectuals and rouse all my old friends against me—the Havets, the Monods, the Bréals. But I do not care a fig for their anathemas and excommunications; I have a higher duty to perform, and I shall perform it. . . . One last question: What does Boisdeffre think of your ideas?"

"Boisdeffre? As soon as I mention the name of Dreyfus in his presence, he changes the subject and starts talking about Russia."

"That's very like him! In conclusion, my dear fellow, remain in as close contact as possible with the General Staff because it is essential that I should be kept well informed. But be continually on your guard."

Friday, January 28, 1898

Dined at the Comtesse Jacques d'Aramon's. There were present D'Annunzio, the Duc and Duchesse de Gramont, the Comtesse René de Béarn, the Comte and Comtesse Arthur de Vogüé.

Mme d'Aramon has long been very friendly with D'Annunzio, whom she often sees in Florence at her sister's, the Contessa Ugolino della Gherardesca. The consequence was that the "child of voluptuousness" did not pose or show off too much this evening because our hostess knew his tricks; he, therefore, resigned himself to being natural, which is all he needs to be charming.

Toward the end of the evening Arthur de Vogüé cornered me and subjected me to the inevitable interrogation about the Dreyfus case.

"The question that I am going to take the liberty of putting to you," he said, "will probably seem to you either absurd or very indiscreet, but I cannot resist the desire to put it to you all the same because I am obsessed by it."

And this acute, skeptical, open-minded man went on to ask me if I believed in the existence of a letter that an agent of Sandherr's was said to have abstracted from the German Embassy in 1894—a letter written to Dreyfus by the Kaiser, which Casimir-Perier was said to have been forced to restore to Münster at the threatening behest of Berlin. A photograph of this letter secretly communicated to the court-martial by General Mercier was said to have led to Dreyfus' conviction.

"As you can imagine," Vogüé went on, "when I read this story in the *Intransigeant* about a month ago, I shrugged my shoulders. But since then I have been assured of its truth in such circumstances and by persons of such standing that I have become very worried. Hence my question. Do you believe in the existence of that letter?"

"What can I answer? Nothing is more difficult to

prove than the non-existence of an imaginary fact. . . .
However, can you imagine the Emperor of Germany,
King of Prussia, Count of Hohenzollern, Margrave of
Brandenburg, Landgrave of Thuringia and of Hesse,
Burgrave of Nuremberg, Duke of Saxony and Pome-
rania, Prince of Nassau—can you imagine his sitting
down at his desk and picking up his pen to write to a
Jewish spy? Is your mind capable for one moment of
entertaining such a fantastic idea?

"Finally, you know M. Casimir-Perier; you know his
proud and ardent patriotism. Can you conceive for a
single moment that he would not indignantly have rejected any threatening demands from Berlin? I can see
him now—how the blood would have sprung to his
cheeks, and how he would have leaped under the outrage. Even at the risk of war, he would have thrown
the German Ambassador out of the room!"

"I don't regret having asked you my question. You
have convinced me. . . . But why do certain people—
people of standing, I repeat—allow the legend to be
believed?"

"That is another matter."

Saturday, January 29, 1898

Dined with Casimir-Perier, in his family circle.

In the course of the evening, he drew me aside and
said:

"I have been summoned to appear as a witness at
the Zola trial on February 7, and I am very worried
about it; I am confronted with a very grave problem
of conscience—a problem that I can confide to hardly

anyone but you. It is this. You will remember that in
1894 I learned from General Mercier that secret documents had been surreptitiously communicated to the
members of the court to support the prosecution, which
was collapsing; there is no doubt in my mind today
that it was those documents that led to the conviction.
If Mercier had consulted me before communicating
those documents to the court, I should certainly have
dissuaded him; for, after all, it was a flagrant violation of the rights of the defense. I shall go further: it
was a crime. But I heard about it only after the verdict.
Should I have informed the Council of Ministers? Perhaps. I admit that at first I did not realize the full im-
plications of the step that Mercier had dared to take.
. . . However that may be, now I have to appear as
a witness at the Assize Court. Have I the right to
disclose something that General Mercier told me in
confidence purely in my capacity as President of the
Republic? Does not the President's Constitutional non-
responsibility impose upon me the duty of keeping silent? . . . That, my dear fellow, is the political and
moral problem that I submit to you. Do not answer immediately because it calls for reflection. But come and
bring me your answer on Monday morning. Could you
not come at nine o'clock, before going to the Ministry?''

"Certainly."

Monday, January 31, 1898

At nine o'clock this morning Casimir-Perier received
me in his study, the big window of which opens on to
the Place des États-Unis.

"Well?" he said, holding out his firm and honest hand. "What is your answer?"

"It is this: As you yourself stated the other day, the clandestine communication of secret documents to the court that tried Dreyfus was a flagrant violation of the rights of the defense and a crime into the bargain, which means that in law the conviction is null and void. However imperative may be the rule of Presidential non-responsibility, you will not be able to keep silent indefinitely about the crime committed by General Mercier. Of that I am certain. But when should you discharge your conscience of this grave secret? Is the time now? Is the Assize Court which is to try Zola really competent to receive such a grave disclosure from you? I think not. In the present inflamed state of people's minds on both sides, both the Dreyfusard and the anti-Dreyfusard, the proceedings in court will certainly be extremely violent. You would thus have to explain yourself in the worst conditions. Moreover, the question at issue at this trial is not Dreyfus' guilt, but Zola's. Now, there are two alternatives. Zola will be either convicted or acquitted. If he is acquitted, the 1894 trial will have to be reopened immediately; if he is convicted, it will have to be reopened a little later on. I assure you that now that is inevitable. Well! it is then that you must speak and tell everything. The *Cour de cassation,* the highest court in France, will require your evidence, and it alone is entitled to relieve you of the Constitutional duty of secrecy."

A light suddenly came into Casimir-Perier's generous face.

"Bravo, my dear fellow!" he said. "I entirely accept your view."

He rose from the armchair in which he was seated near me, sat at his desk, picked up his pen, and drafted a letter to the president of the Assize Court.

I know of no facts relevant to the case with which the court is now vested. If I were to be examined about events that took place when I was President of the Republic, the doctrine of Constitutional non-responsibility would impose silence on me.

After a moment's reflection, he added:

However, out of respect to the court, I am ready to repeat this declaration in front of it.

Tuesday, February 2, 1898

In the Italian Parliament yesterday, Count Bonin, the Foreign Under-Secretary of State, said:

"I declare in the most explicit fashion that neither our military attaché nor any other agent of the Italian Government has ever had any dealings, direct or indirect, with the former Captain Dreyfus."

Saturday, February 5, 1898

Lunched at Mme Aubernon de Nerville's. There were present D'Annunzio, Paul Hervieu, the Baronne de Pierrebourg, Louis Ganderax and Mme Ganderax,

Gregh, Mme Laure Baignères, Mme Straus, the Marquis du Tillet, etc.

No sooner were we seated at table than Mme Aubernon started harassing D'Annunzio.

"Oh, please tell us quickly what your method is in love!" she said. "What do you think of concupiscence, chastity, caprice, adultery, jealousy, childbirth, infidelity ... ?"

D'Annunzio tried to reply. But soon, overwhelmed by the avalanche of absurd questions, he pointed to the steaming eggs on his plate and, in a quiet, firm, but respectful, manner, said to his hostess:

"Oh, Madam, read my books and let me get on with my lunch!"

All the guests started, and there was a deathly silence.

When D'Annunzio had finished his eggs, he became more conciliatory, and the conversation livened up again; everyone played his part, if only out of pity for our hostess; and D'Annunzio, his feathers no longer ruffled, lent himself with perfect grace and simplicity to the conversational firework-display that was expected of him. Here are some of the things he said: "You asked me just now what my method was in love, Madam. It is silence and action." ... "I have never known either remorse or regret; I live only in the present; I perpetually need new pleasures and new sensations." ... "Being *immoral?* What could be more simple! Anybody can be *immoral*. But only a genius can be *moral*." ... "Lying is the necessary ornament of life; it is the only thing that makes it tolerable." ... "Since

the beginning of my adolescence, I have been drunk
with voluptuousness!''

At this point, Mme Aubernon interrupted him. ''How
sorry I am for you,'' she said, ''I, who have always
been drunk with chastity!''

Before leaving the table D'Annunzio's health was
drunk.

''To your success!'' . . . ''To your speedy return
among us! etc., etc.''

Paul Hervieu, who had remained taciturn throughout lunch because he dislikes D'Annunzio's gifts and
finds him personally revolting, said coldly:

''To your glory!''

While coffee was being served Mme Straus [7] drew
me into a corner of the drawing-room.

''Come and sit down,'' she said to me. ''I want to
talk to you confidentially. . . . You know that my husband and I are very friendly with Princess Mathilde.
We go to her every Wednesday; she comes to us nearly
every Saturday.[8] Well, since the Dreyfus case has come

[7] Mme Straus, born in 1846, was the daughter of the composer
Fromenthal Halévy and cousin of the writer Ludovic Halévy. In
1865 she married Georges Bizet. After his death she married Émile
Straus, the great commercial lawyer who was counsel for the Roths-
childs. At her house in the Rue de Miromesnil she held a *salon* that
was frequented, among others, by Princess Mathilde, Victorien
Sardou, Maupassant, Georges de Porto-Riche, Abel Hermant, Marcel
Prévost, and Paul Hervieu.

[8] Princess Mathilde Bonaparte (1820–1904), daughter of Jérôme,
one time King of Westphalia, had once nearly married her cousin,
Louis Napoleon. In 1841 she married a Russian, Anatole Demidoff,
Prince of San Donato, from whom she separated in 1845. Her *salon*,
both before and after 1870, was one of the principal meeting-places

up again, there has been a slight coldness, or rather a slight feeling of embarrassment, between us. The princess is a passionate anti-Dreyfusard, and my husband and I believe Dreyfus to be innocent. But as the princess is frankness and honesty itself, and as she is very fond of us, she is very grieved at our 'mistake'; and not a week passes without her trying to convert us. Thus one day, about two months ago now, she called and found me alone by the fireside and said to me: 'Do you still believe in Dreyfus' innocence?' 'More than ever, princess,' I answered. 'Well! you should know that there is irrefutable evidence against him. I have it from General de Boisdeffre himself that the General Staff has managed to lay its hands on some letters written to Dreyfus by the Kaiser; and there is no doubt about their authenticity. Is that enough for you?' I was very upset by this and asked Princess Mathilde if she would be good enough to repeat to my husband what she had just told me. 'But of course!' she said. 'If he's here, let him come!' I immediately sent for my husband, who was in his study, and the princess repeated to him exactly what she had said to me. . . . That is what I wanted to tell you. I know that you are concerned with the Dreyfus case; people even say that you know the inside story. So I beg and implore you to tell me frankly: do you believe in the existence of the letters that General de Boisdeffre told Princess Mathilde about?''

---

of the literary and artistic world. It was frequented by Renan, Sainte-Beuve, Taine, Flaubert, the Goncourt brothers, and later by Maupassant, Bourget, Léon Daudet, and Anatole France.

I had no hesitation in replying:

"If a single letter from the Kaiser to Dreyfus is in existence, I shall be perfectly willing to believe in the existence of a number of them. But until I have held a single such letter in my hands and carefully checked its authenticity, I shall never believe that H.M. the Emperor of Germany and King of Prussia has ever been in correspondence with a spy."

"Oh! how happy I am to hear you!" [9]

[9] *Author's note:* Instinctively I do not like the Jews; but I profoundly object to anti-Semitism because I see only too clearly its iniquities, aberrations, and wickedness.

However, I cannot forget an idea that the broad-minded Renan, that ardent admirer of the history of Jewish ideas, has several times developed in his Sunday receptions at the Collège de France and that could no doubt be found in his writings; the idea that, "religious intolerance, religious exclusiveness, comes to us directly from the Hebrew Bible, for the Greeks and Romans know nothing of theological fanaticism; and that Ximenes and Torquemada are the continuers of Isaiah and Jeremiah." *Patere legem quam ipse fecisti!*

Paul Bourget, who regards me as a Dreyfusard, recently quoted me a page of Renan, drawn from *l'Ecclésiaste,* which is indeed rather hard for the Jews of our day:

Cohelet is above all the modern Jew. From him to Heinrich Heine there is only a door to be pushed ajar. Wait two thousand years for the pride of Rome to have been exhausted, for babarism to have passed away; you will see how this son of the prophets, this cousin of Christ, has turned out to be an accomplished worldling, how heedless he is of a paradise that the world believed in on his word, how easily he fits into the folds of modern society, how he enjoys a world he did not make, gathers the fruits of a field he did not labor, supplants the idler who persecutes him, makes himself necessary to the fool who despises him. You would think it was for him that Clovis and his Franks struck such mighty blows with their swords, that the race of Capet conquered at Bouvines and Condé at Rocroy. . . . O vanity of vanities! . . . We have all known him, the worldly sage led astray by no supernatural chimeras, who would give all the dreams of another world for the realities of an hour of this one; who is greatly opposed to abuses and is, nevertheless, as little demorcratic as possible; is simultaneously supple and proud

Monday, February 7, 1898

Today was the first day of the trial of Zola arising out
of his letter to the President of the Republic entitled
J'Accuse! [10]

The president of the Assize Court is Délegorgue; the
prosecution is in the hands of Van Cassel, the Advocate-General. Zola is defended by Maître Labori; and
Maître Albert Clemenceau, the brother of the poli-

---

if he has power; is aristocratic by reason of his nervous sensibility and
his attitude of one who has succeeded in setting aside exhausting labor;
is bourgeois because of his slight esteem for warlike valor and the age-
long abasement from which his distinction does not save him. He who
changed the world by his belief in the kingdom of God no longer believes
in anything but riches. No crazy chivalry makes him exchange his lux-
urious abode for glory dangerously acquired. In his view the whole
content of life is here below. . . . A surprising confirmation of the
philosophy of vanity! Disturb the whole world, let God die on the cross,
endure every torture, have your country destroyed three or four times
by fire, insult all the tyrants, upset all their idols, and end up by dying
of a spinal complaint in a well-appointed mansion in the Champs-
Élysées quarter regretting that life is so short and pleasure so fleeting.
O vanity of vanities!—*l'Ecclésiaste.*

[10] Zola's open letter to the President of the Republic appeared on
January 13, 1898, in Clemenceau's newspaper the *Aurore.* Clenmen-
ceau was a friend of Zola and had suggested to him the title of the
letter, which was a violent diatribe against the "illegalities, frauds,
and juridical crimes of the General Staff." Zola wrote in his sum-
ming up:

*I accuse General Mercier of having made himself an accomplice, at
any rate out of weakness of spirit, of one of the greatest iniquities of
the century.*

*I accuse General Billot of having had in his hands positive proofs of
Dreyfus' innocence and of having stifled them, of having made himself
guilty of this crime against humanity and justice for a political purpose and to save the compromised General Staff.*

*I accuse General de Boisdeffre and General Gonse of having made
themselves accomplices in the same crime, the former no doubt because
of clerical passion, the latter because of that* esprit de corps *that makes
the offices of the War Department the holy of holies, unassailable, etc.*

tician, is appearing for Perreux, the manager of the
Aurore.

The whole hearing was taken up with the usual formalities: selection of the jury by lot, calling of witnesses, reading of preliminary documents, etc.

A journalist who came from the Palais de Justice
told me:

"You can imagine that the court was crammed, even
to the window sills. And what passion there was on people's faces! What looks of hatred when certain eyes
met! Outside, the *Libre Parole* gangs applauded the
generals and hissed the Dreyfusards. If the police
don't take stricter measures tomorrow, there will be
violence."

"Did you see Esterhazy?"

"Oh, yes, I saw him. . . . All eyes were fixed on him,
but nobody shook hands with him. The officers had actually been forbidden to talk to him. He wandered alone
between the groups, looking haggard and ferocious.
What a fine type of rogue!"

Tuesday, February 8, 1898

Second day of the Zola trial.

Casimir-Perier appeared and said: "I have come
here only out of respect for the court. I cannot in fact
take the oath to speak the whole truth, for if I were
asked about events that took place while I was President of the Republic, silence would be imposed on me
by the Constitutional principle of non-responsibility."

During the evening Casimir-Perier telephoned me.

"I want to tell you that everything passed off very

well," he said. "My 'Constitutional' excuse roused no
protests. . . . On the way out the Dreyfusards applauded me, which was probably an indirect way of
demonstrating against my successor. . . . I've just been
told that there have been terrible brawls in the Rue de
Harlay and the Place Dauphine. When Yves Guyot,
Reinach, and Zola left the Palais, they were set on by
a huge crowd yelling: 'Into the water with the traitors!' and 'Death to the Jews!' The Prefect of Police
had to intervene in person to rescue them."

Wednesday, February 16, 1898

The Zola trial has been going for nine days, but it is
far from over. I made three brief visits to the court
in order to have at least a picture of it in my mind.

As soon as the case opened, the court ruled the proceedings would be restricted to consideration of the
complaint by the Minister of War, that is to say the
alleged libel of the members of the court that tried
Esterhazy. The Advocate-General warned the accused
and their counsel that "we shall not under any pretext
whatever permit a reopening of the question of the
verdict of 1894; the *res judicata* will be respected. If
any attempt is made insidiously to provoke a reopening of the case, the court will not lend itself to it."

That is what has been done. Whenever the lawyers
asked a leading question, the president promptly
stopped them in the dryest tone with the peremptory
formula: "The question will not be put." I doubt
whether the annals of the Restoration or the Second
Empire contain an example of a political trial in which

the Government's orders were more rigorously carried out.

All the chief figures in the drama appeared on the scene:

Zola, nervous, sullen, sheepish, letting fall clumsy phrases such as: "I don't know the law, and I don't want to know it" or, "I have gained by my works more victories than the generals who insult me; I have carried the French language to the ends of the earth!"

General Mercier, haughty, phlegmatic, severe, precise, superciliously entrenched in awareness of his infallibility, hurling at the jury this terrible parting shot: "We have not the right to reopen the 1894 trial. But if we had to return to it, and I were asked for my word as a soldier, I should swear once more that Dreyfus was a traitor and was rightly and legally convicted!"

Mathieu Dreyfus and his sister-in-law, *Mme Lucie Dreyfus,* both very dignified, inspiring everybody with compassion, or at any rate respect.

General de Boisdeffre, who in the public eye is the embodiment of responsibility for the national defense and the secrets of the Russian alliance, very distinguished in manner, calm without stiffness, neatly evading all dangerous questions and concluding his testimony, like General Mercier, with this solemn declaration: "In 1894 there was no doubt in my mind about the guilt of Captain Dreyfus. Innumerable pieces of evidence that have since come to us have made my certainty unshakable."

Trarieux, the former Keeper of the Seals, a man of

the greatest integrity, almost Jansenist in his austerity, a fervent advocate of reopening the case, but too naive in appearance, too emphatic, too verbose, expressing himself only in commonplaces, and thus losing all hold on his hearers.[11]

Colonel du Paty de Clam, pretentious, monocle in eye, well set-up, abrupt in speech, and with mechanical gestures; a disturbing character, with a morbid mentality, a shadowy and unhinged imagination, a strange mixture of fanaticism, extravagance, and folly; it would not be surprising to find him in a ''Tale of Hoffman.'' [12]

[11] Jacques Trarieux (1840–1904), a lawyer by profession, was a deputy from 1879 to 1881, and then a senator for the Gironde. Alexandre Ribot entrusted him with the Ministry of Justice in his second Cabinet (January-November, 1895). He was the founder and first president of the League of the Rights of Man.

[12] Ferdinand du Paty de Clam, born 1853, was the son of General du Paty de Clam (1813–1887). He enlisted at the age of seventeen in the 106th Bataillon de Marche formed during the siege of Paris. In 1877, after passing through St. Cyr and the staff college, he was the youngest captain in the army. After serving in the Tunisian campaign and on the staff of the 17th Army Corps at Toulouse, he was transferred to the Third Bureau of the General Staff with the rank of major. The Dreyfus case broke his career. He was retired in 1900 with the rank of lieutenant-colonel.

In 1914, at the age of sixty-one, he enlisted as a rifleman, second class, in the 16th Bataillon de Chasseurs à Pied in the company commanded by his eldest son, with which he fought before Conflans. He was recalled to employment in his old rank, posted to the 17th Regiment of Infantry, and was seriously wounded at the end of September, 1914. He rejoined his unit before his wound was healed, led his battalion to the victorious assault and recapture of Quesnoy-en-Santerre on October 30, 1914, and died as a result of his wounds on September 3, 1916.

General Gonse, a worthy man, a glutton for work, but weak, timorous, and indecisive . . . and really too stupid.

Lieutenant-Colonel Henry, solid, sturdy, and thickset, with florid cheeks and open features concealing plenty of cunning beneath his rude, frank exterior.

Major Lauth, tall, slender, frigid, reticent, extremely intelligent, secretive, the intimate collaborator, not to say the chief, of his chief, Henry.

Lieutenant-Colonel Picquart, tall and slim, with a rather stiff distinction, high forehead, eyes rather difficult to catch between his close eyebrows, expressing himself precisely, but obviously embarrassed in his behavior by the ferocious hatred of his comrades and perhaps even more by the delirious praise lavished on him by the fanatics of Dreyfusism, torn between the duties of professional discipline, on the one hand, and the risks of open rebellion, on the other, rather like a priest who, having gone astray in a theological controversy, felt hovering over his head the thunderbolts of anathema and excommunication.

General de Pellieux, superbly bold and plucky and a fine fencer, having not the slightest shadow of doubt about Dreyfus' guilt, and putting forth in the service of his belief the ardor, eloquence, and intrepidity of a believer testifying to his creed.

The archivist Gribelin, gentle, modest, self-effacing, the perfect servant, monastic in his docility, *perinde ac cadaver*. He could say a lot if he wanted to, for all the machinations of the intelligence department pass through his hands; it is he who registers documents, classifies them, keeps the files, makes payments, holds the keys of the ark and the tabernacle.

I nearly forgot the *handwriting experts,* absurd creatures incapable of agreeing on the most elementary deductions, flinging their extraordinary theories in one another's faces and running down and abusing one another like Molière's doctors. But one of them deserves special mention—Bertillon, who is a madman, a maniac, armed with the crafty, obstinate, and powerful dialectic that is the characteristic of interpretative psychosis.

As for the proceedings themselves, they are nothing but a long sequence of altercations and violent speeches, constantly interrupted by the automatic refrain of the president of the court: "The question will not be put!"

Thursday, February 17, 1898

According to police information which reached the War Ministry yesterday, the Assize Court jury, exhausted by the interminable arguments, in the course of which, moreover, they felt that the truth was eluding them, were inclining to acquit Zola.

General de Pellieux, who has definitely become the spokesman of the General Staff, accordingly felt that the hour had come to strike, and strike home.

On the pretext of desiring to supplement his previous evidence, he suddenly leaped toward the bar and declared in ringing tones:

"Dreyfus' crime is established by one piece of ir-

refutable evidence, which I have seen and held in my
own hands. It is a letter addressed by a foreign military attaché to his colleague in another country. You
will guess who it is of whom I speak. This is what the
letter contains: 'I learn that there is to be an interpellation in the Chamber on the Dreyfus case. Never admit
the dealings we have had with this Jew.' . . . I appeal
to General de Boisdeffre to confirm what I have just
said!''

This disclosure let loose such a violent tumult, such
a din of applause, on the one hand, and anger, on the
other, that the court adjourned until tomorrow to hear
General de Boisdeffre.

Friday, February 18, 1898

At half-past two this afternoon, on the Quai d'Orsay
on my way to the Ministry, I saw in front of me Lieutenant-Colonel Henry, walking in the direction of the
Esplanade des Invalides. For a moment I was not sure
that it was he, for he looked different from his usual
self. He was walking slowly, hesitantly, and his back
was bent.

I overtook him and tapped him on the shoulder. He
turned abruptly. His face frightened me. He was hol-
low-cheeked and pale, and his eyes were drawn and feverish.

''What's the matter with you, my dear colonel? Are
you ill? You look bad!''

''Oh, I had an attack of my Tonkin fever again last
night—a terrible attack. The result is that I can hardly

stand up. But I had to go to the Assize Court, where General de Boisdeffre has just confirmed General de Pellieux's evidence. I left immediately afterward; I was feeling too ill to stay any longer. Now I'm going home to put myself to bed."

"Would you like me to walk a little way with you?"

"Certainly! But I shan't be able to tell you much. I'm feeling terrible, and my head is bursting."

Nevertheless it was he who started the conversation.

"What a day's hearing it was yesterday!" he said. "By ... ! I haven't got over it yet!"

"You're referring to the Pellieux incident?"

"I certainly am! What Pellieux did was absurd! Documents as secret as that should not be disclosed in public."

"What? Do you mean to say General de Pellieux did not consult General Gonse or General de Boisdeffre before carrying out his *coup de théâtre?*"

"No! What happened was this. During an adjournment, General de Pellieux called Gribelin and said to him: 'You have a good memory, Gribelin? . . . Then repeat to me Panizzardi's letter to Schwartzkoppen—the letter that ends with the words: "Never admit that we have had dealings with this Jew." ' Gribelin repeated the letter to him word for word, without suspecting the use the general was going to make of it. Then the court resumed, and without consulting anybody, General de Pellieux asked permisison to supplement his evidence. I was sitting next to General Gonse; we looked at each other in amazement. What on earth could Pellieux be going to say now? He advanced to

the bar and repeated the letter, word for word. Gonse
whispered into my ear: 'There! You heard that? What
a fool!' As for myself, it took my breath away. . . .
I'm sure it was that that gave me my attack of fever."

By this time we had passed the Boulevard de la
Tour-Maubourg and were starting to walk down the
Avenue de la Motte-Picquet. I said to Henry:

"You genuinely have no doubt about the authenticity
of the Panizzardi letter?"

"None whatever."

"But you remember Tornielli's recent categorical
and official statement that if Dreyfus is mentioned
either by name or by any other description in a letter
attributed to Panizzardi, that letter is bogus."

"But I've told you often enough that the authenticity of the document is demonstrated by a large
number of similar documents!"

We had now reached the corner of the Avenue Du-
quesne, where Henry lives. There I left him to go to
the Ministry.

Nisard, to whom I promptly reported this conversation, shut his eyes for a moment, as he does when he
is concentrating his admirable intuitive faculties. Then,
looking at me with that sharp look of his, he said:

"That document is bogus."

Wednesday, February 23, 1898

The trial of Zola, after going on for fifteen days with
continually increasing violence, has ended at last. The
triumph of the General Staff can be said to have been

certain ever since General de Pellieux's last intervention, or rather his last charge.

Zola has been sentenced to the maximum penalty, a year's imprisonment and a fine of three thousand francs, and Perreux, a simple accomplice, came off with four months' imprisonment and the same fine.

From Saturday, March 5 to Sunday, March 20, 1898 Trip to Rome.

The Italians are nearly as stirred by the Dreyfus case as are the French, but with the difference that here nobody believes Dreyfus to be guilty. People here do not understand how it is that it has not long since become obvious to the normally so quick and discriminating French mind that the 1894 verdict, the result of a genuine judicial error, was the result of a gigantic imposture. That is the impression I have gathered at the Duca di Sermoneta's, at the Contessa Pasolini's, at Signora Mazzoleni's, at the Contessa Bruschi's, at the Marchese Visconti-Venosta's, at the Duchessa Grazioli's, in fact everywhere; and that impression has been fully confirmed by Barrère, our Ambassador. D'Annunzio himself, who hates the Jews, said to me during one of our walks on the Palatine:

"There's no doubt about it. This time Judas is innocent!"

In Vatican circles a different state of mind prevails. Here they avoid committing themselves on the crux of the matter, the question whether Dreyfus was legally and rightly convicted, but an insidious tenacity is

shown in letting slip no opportunity of expressing pity
for poor France, which is now discovering to its cost
the ordeals and perils to which a nation exposes itself
when it allows itself to be governed by Freemasons,
atheists, and Jews!

Wednesday, April 20, 1898

Lieutenant-Colonel Henry has just brought me his
weekly tribute of information. He was very cheerful
today, fresh-cheeked and with a sparkle in his eye.

"First of all," he said, "General Gonse asked me to
send you his kind regards. He complains that he has
been seeing too little of you. In these times, one can't
see one's friends often enough!"

"My dear colonel, that is an opening that bodes no
good. You're dangling a carrot in front of me; you're
going to ask me for more money!"

"Money, no! But it's true that I'm going to ask you
for something."

He explained that the Minister of War had instructed General de Boisdeffre to collect all the documents relating to the Dreyfus case into a single file and
classify them systematically. Now, in carrying out this
task Lieutenant-Colonel Henry had been unable to find
the celebrated telegram sent by Panizzardi on November 2, 1894, and he had come to ask me "as a personal
favor" to supply him with a duplicate.

I started.

"What!" I exclaimed. "You can't find the telegram
of November 2, 1894! Come, Henry! A document as important as that doesn't get lost!"

"No, of course not, we didn't lose it," he stammered. "But we've looked for it everywhere and can't find it. . . . There are so many documents connected with the case. . . . And then you remember how ill poor Sandherr was when he left the service. Where did he put that telegram? How should I know?"

This story seemed to me so suspicious that I answered:

"I'm sorry, my dear colonel, but I don't think I am entitled to hand you a document of that nature without an official request from General Billot."

Henry insisted:

"Come!" he said. "Be decent to us!"

"Oh, no! On matters like this I am not to be got round. But I've repeated the text of that telegram to you so often that I don't mind doing so again. You are free to write it down to my dictation."

He took a pen and a piece of paper, and I dictated to him: "If Captain Dreyfus has not had dealings with you, it would be advisable to instruct the Ambassador to publish an official denial to avoid comments in the press."

Henry rose to his feet. But no trace of his recent cheerfulness remained. He looked upset. With his hand on the door-handle he said:

"This may be the last time I shall come to see you."

"Why?"

"I've asked for a transfer from the intelligence service."

"What is the matter with you?"

"What is the matter with me is that I've had enough

of the damned service. You get nothing but troubles, and not a day's rest. . . . Besides, I'm not a chair cushion, I'm a soldier, I like regimental life, life with the men, life in the open air. . . . And besides, as I've told you, I've had enough, enough, by G. . . !''

Nisard, to whom I immediately described this strange visit, with his usual swiftness, said to me:

"We are reaching the crux of the drama. *Ad eventum festinamus*, as Horace would have said."

Thursday, April 21, 1898

Spain and the United States have broken off diplomatic relations.[13]

In the dispute which is thus ending in war, Hanotaux seems to me to have come out a little too openly in favor of the Spaniards, who are beaten in advance. But, after all the Queen Regent [14] and the Emperor Francis Joseph have overwhelmed him with compliments, and have had him informed that he holds the fate of the Spanish monarchy in his hands! How could the historian of Richelieu, the panegyrist of the great enemy of the House of Austria, have failed to be flattered and won over? . . . That was the vivid impression I had in dining in his company this evening at the Princesse de Wagram's, where as usual he was the subject of much adulation.

When we left, he said to me:

"Can I give you a lift home, my dear fellow?"

[13] Over Cuba.
[14] Maria Christina (1858–1929) was the widow of Alfonso XII and the mother of Alfonso XIII, who in 1898 was aged twelve.

He made me get into his carriage. I told him about my conversation with Lieutenant-Colonel Henry yesterday and my refusal to give him a duplicate of the Panizzardi telegram.

"Oh, how I approve of what you did!" Hanotaux said. "How could they let a document as important as that go astray? They have destroyed it, don't you think?"

"That's what I'm wondering. . . . For what is this file that they are collecting, or tampering with, *in extremis?* And why does Henry want to leave the intelligence service? . . . It's all very suspicious."

"Yes, it's even frightening. So be on your guard more than ever, my dear fellow."

Saturday, April 23, 1898

Lunched at the Comtesse d'Haussonville's. Present were her husband,[15] her brother, Emmanuel d'Harcourt, Pierre Loti, Georges de Porto-Riche, Dr. Pozzi.[16]

[15] Othenin, Comte d'Haussonville (1843–1924), was on his mother's side a great-grandson of Mme de Staël; his mother was born a Broglie. He was an Orléanist deputy in the National Assembly and collaborated with his uncle, the Duc de Broglie. He took an active part in the negotiations between Orleanists and Legitimists with a view to "fusion" and a restoration. After the victory of the Republicans in the elections of 1877, he abandoned public life and devoted himself to literary history and social studies. In 1883, after the death of the Comte de Chambord, he returned to politics and became one of the principal advisers of the Comte de Paris. On the prince's death in 1894, he gave up all political activity. His wife Pauline d'Harcourt, Comtesse d'Haussonville (1846–1922) had a literary and political *salon.*

[16] Samuel Pozzi (1846–1918) was a celebrated surgeon, and Professor of Clinical Gynecology in the Faculty of Medicine.

At table we talked about the hostilities which have
just begun between Spain and the United States; the
chances of the two belligerents were estimated, and
our prognostications were not in favor of Spain.

I said to Pierre Loti:

"Is it true that you are going to serve with the Spanish Fleet?"

"Yes, I leave for Madrid this evening; but I am very
embarrassed. I am willing to give two or three months
of my life to the Spanish cause, but two years, no!
Now, the war may last two years. Another thing is,
what will they do with me? My dignity permits me to
accept nothing less than a command. I mistrust the
ship that they will give me; the engines, the guns, the
tackle, everything will be faulty. I know the Spanish
navy! Can you see me failing in an operation or being
captured by the Americans because of a boiler break-
down? I should cover myself with ridicule! But never
mind! I shall go and see the Queen Regent, assure her
of my sympathy, and ask her advice."

How all this affectation, this ingenuousness, this
play-acting, this obsession with playing a role and making a dramatic impact fits in with poor Loti's reddened
cheeks, blued eyelids, lengthened eyebrows—his whole
made-up face! To get me to forgive these faults—to
say nothing of others—all the magic of *Rarahu* and
Aziyadé is not too much.

When Dr. Pozzi, who is always in a hurry, gave the
signal for departure at about two o'clock, D'Haussonville whispered to me:

"Please don't go for a few minutes; my wife, Emmanual, and I are conspiring to ask you a very indiscreet question.''

All four of us sat down again by the fireplace. Mme d'Haussonville, with that frankness of language and manner that makes her friendship so delightful, then said:

''We have learned from a very good source that it is you who deal with the Dreyfus case at the Quai d'Orsay. Therefore, as Othenin, Emmanuel, and I have great confidence in you, we have decided to ask you under the seal of secrecy whether or not you believe Dreyfus to be guilty.''

D'Haussonville went on:

''We wish you to understand this, my dear fellow. We do not ask you to tell us the reasons that make you believe that Dreyfus is guilty or innocent because you could not tell us those without breaking the most elementary rules of official discretion; all we want to know is the opinion to which you have come as a result of reading and handling the files. Since we are talking openly, I shall even tell you how I found out that it is you who deal with the case at the Quai d'Orsay; your chief, Hanotaux, said so the other day at the Academy, in Poincaré's presence and my own.''

D'Haussonville, whose rather dry exterior covers a great fund of charity,[17] went on to tell me that he was gravely troubled by the Dreyfus case.

[17] The Comte d'Haussonville undertook numerous investigations of social problems, the results of which were incorporated in his *l'Enfance à Paris* (1879); *Misères et remèdes* (1892); *Socialisme et charité* (1895); *Salaires et misères de femmes* (1900). He was president of the Philanthropic Society and of the Society for the Protection of Alsatians and Lorrainers.

"The idea of an innocent man in prison is intolerable
to me," he went on, "and I shall never admit that a
Jew has not the same right as any Christian to all the
guarantees of the law. These doctrines of hatred and
outlawry revolt me; it is not for nothing that I am
the great-grandson of Mme de Staël. As for the brutal
anti-Semitic demonstrations that we have just seen at
Lunéville, Épinal, Bordeaux, Toulouse, Grenoble and
throughout Algeria, they fill my heart with disgust.
. . . On the other hand, the campaign that the Dreyfusards and their great ally, M. Jaurès, have undertaken
against the army is abominable. What General de Pellieux recently said at the Assize Court was very true:
'In destroying the confidence that the army must have
in its leaders, you destroy the army itself.' What will
become of our unhappy soldiers when they are led into
action by generals whom they have been taught to despise? On that day M. Zola will be able to write another *Débâcle*. Once more he will carry the French language to the ends of the earth, but on the world map
you will search in vain for the name of France!"
He concluded:
"That, my dear fellow, is what we have been continually talking about between ourselves; for me personally the question has become agonizing. . . . Could
you not, in strict confidence, throw a little light on it
for us?"
"I feel no hesitation in answering you," I said, "because I am sure that my answer will go no farther than
these four walls. In 1894 I firmly believed in Dreyfus'
guilt; now I am doubtful about it."
D'Harcourt exclaimed in astonishment:

"But the letter which General de Pellieux quoted in the Assize Court and General de Boisdeffre confirmed! Doesn't that seem to you to be decisive?"

"I have not seen the document. I, therefore, cannot give you any guarantee of its authenticity."

All three started at once and exclaimed:

"But then ... !"

Thursday, June 30, 1898

The Méline Cabinet, which has just been overthrown for having leaned too far to the Right, has been succeeded by a Cabinet led by Brisson.[18] The War Ministry has gone to Cavaignac[19] and the Ministry of Foreign Affairs to Delcassé.[20]

[18] Henri Brisson, born at Bourges in 1835, was deputy for Paris from 1871 onward and for Marseilles from 1902 onward. He was a high dignitary in Freemasonry and was one of the leading personalities of the Radical Party. He was three times president of the Chamber: from 1881 to 1885, from 1894 to 1898, and from 1904 until his death in 1912. He was Prime Minister for the first time from April to December, 1885. In the Cabinet he formed on June 28, 1898, he was Minister of the Interior in addition to Prime Minister. This Cabinet remained in office until November 2 of the same year.

[19] Godefroy Cavaignac, born in 1853, was a member of a famous republican family. He was Minister of Marine in 1892 and was now War Minister for the second time: he had held this portfolio in the Government of Léon Bourgeois from November, 1895 to April, 1896. He enjoyed a great reputation for integrity, and confidence was felt that he would study the Dreyfus file and proclaim the truth, whatever it might be.

[20] Théophile Delcassé, deputy for l'Ariège since 1889, had been Minister for the Colonies in the Dupuy Cabinet of 1894. The Foreign

Saturday, July 2, 1898

Spent two long hours with my new Minister going through the secret file on the Franco-Russian alliance. Nisard was present. ....

:...

:...

When Nisard withdrew, Delcassé asked me to remain; he wanted to question me about the Dreyfus case. By way of introduction, he said:

"Talk to me with complete frankness; I shall be equally frank with you. We shall have to work together a great deal; I know you are worthy of all my confidence, so grant me yours."

I described to him how I had come to believe the 1894 trial was a put-up job, organized by subordinates to cover those really guilty of treason; and I added that most of the documents used to incriminate Dreyfus seemed to me to be either apocryphal or, at any rate, highly suspect. Delcassé sat still and silent while I talked, and when I had finished he said:

"You mentioned 'those really guilty.' So there are several?"

"That is what I think."

"I do not ask you whom you suspect because you have mentioned no names."

"I have mentioned no names because there is still too much uncertainty and conjecture about my suspicions."

Affairs portfolio which Brisson entrusted to him on June 28, 1898, remained uninterruptedly in his hands until June 12, 1905.

"I approve of your atitude. But I want to know your
view of the role of General de Boisdeffre and General
Gonse."

"They are dupes in the matter."

"But Boisdeffre is very intelligent."

"Boisdeffre, yes. But he is easy-going, dislikes trouble, and is terribly afraid of abuse in the Nationalist
press; the slightest attack, the slightest criticism, by
Rochefort or Drumont throws him into a panic. I imagine that he must long ago have suspected the gangre-
nous growth underlying the Dreyfus case, but that he
lacks the courage for the necessary surgical operation,
which henceforth it will be impossible to avoid."

In conclusion Delcassé confirmed the instructions
given to me by Hanotaux: to remain in close contact
with the General Staff, but studiously to avoid anything that might involve the Quai d'Orsay in the tan-
gled enigma of the Dreyfus case.

Thursday, July 7, 1898

There was a pathetic session of the Chamber; Cavaignac, incidentally in very noble language, devoted himself to a demonstration of Dreyfus' guilt by disclosing
all the evidence.

He started by summarily condemning Esterhazy for
all the disgraceful details of his private life, but he
justified his acquittal of the crime of 1894.

Then, beginning his demonstration, he went on:

"No reason of public security, however high, could
ever persuade me to keep an innocent man in jail."

Having thus draped himself in his proud and rigid integrity, he went on coldly to produce his evidence—the statement signed by Captain Lebrun-Renaud alleging Dreyfus' confession, a number of General Staff memoranda, and finally three documents from the arch-secret file, including the famous letter specifically mentioning Dreyfus' name, already produced by General de Pellieux. He spoke about each document in peremptory and dogmatic fashion, guaranteeing its indubitable authenticity and ended with a fine peroration in honor of the army.

When he came down from the rostrum, the whole House gave him a delirious standing ovation. The House voted unanimously that the speech should be posted up in public places.[21] There were, however, sixteen abstentions—those of the fifteen Socialists, about which there was nothing surprising, and that of old Méline. As prudent as Nestor, as subtle as Ulysses.

Eugène-Melchoir de Vogüé, to whom I talked this evening at the club, said:

"Now the odious case is buried! Now Dreyfus is nailed to his rock till he dies!"

Thursday, August 26, 1898

A grave incident has just arisen in Franco-Russian relations.

Yesterday morning Count Muraviev, the Czar's Foreign Minister, asked our Ambassador, the Marquis de Montebello, to call in connection with an urgent

[21] *I.e.,* outside the town hall in every French commune.

matter. He said: "I desire you to be the first to be acquainted with an important decision of his Majesty's which I have to communicate this afternoon to your foreign colleagues. For some time the Emperor has been worried, even alarmed, at the fashion in which all countries are developing their military strength. He believes that the risk of war is thus growing from day to day, and that, if the present situation continues, it will inevitably lead to a cataclysm the horror of which makes him tremble in advance. He has, therefore, decided to invite all governments to meet at an international conference for the purpose of devising ways and means of reducing the excessive armaments, which are a burden to the nations, and of assuring the world the benefit of universal peace. Such a conference would, God willing, be a very happy augury for the new century which is about to begin."

Muraviev's constrained manner and the brevity of his explanations made it immediately plain to Montebello that this initiative of the Czar's did not have the approval of his Foreign Minister. Muraviev, indeed, had no part either in the conception or in the details of the project that he had received instructions to carry out. The originator of the idea is the celebrated Pobedonostsev, Chief Procurator of the Holy Synod, who, having been the friend and confidant of the "most pious" Alexander III, has become the political instructor and all-powerful adviser of Nicholas II.[22] Thus, in

[22] Konstantine Petrovich Pobedonostsev (1827–1907) had been Professor of Law at Moscow University, a senator, a member of the Imperial Council, and finally a tutor of Alexander III. The latter

this matter which implies a major transformation in
international affairs, it was not even suggested that
diplomacy might have a word to say. That is why Russia's ally, France, was not consulted; the Russians
confined themselves to informing the French representative a few hours before all the other ambassadors
and ministers.

How will Delcassé react?

The news surprised him at his estate at Ariège,
where he had gone for a rest; he is returning immediately to Paris.

Monday, August 29, 1898

The rescript announced by Muraviev was promulgated
yesterday.

Delcassé, who has just returned to Paris, sent for
me this afternoon to study the whole genesis of the alliance with him and to search for arguments to use
with the Russian Government with a view to attenuating as far as possible the untoward effects of the imperial initiative.

His drawn features, his yellowish complexion, his
nervous gestures, his jerky speech, revealed his state
of mind only too plainly.

"What the Emperor has just done is sheer mad-

---

made him his intimate confidant and friend, and upon his accession
in 1881 appointed him Procurator General of the Holy Synod, that
is to say, the Czar's representative in the supreme council of the
Russian Church. Pobedonostsev was fanatically Orthodox and a
partisan of the absolute autocracy of the Czars. He earned himself
the nickname of "Grand Inquisitor of Holy Russia," and inspired
the whole of Alexander III's anti-liberal policy.

ness!" he said. "How can he have engaged in a diplomatic enterprise of such enormous compass, having such profound and widespread repercussions, without first assuring himself of our consent? Was the Franco-Russian alliance designed only to procure from us, under the pretext of philanthropy, a solemn confirmation of the Treaty of Frankfurt? Look how exultant the German press is! Look at its interminable eulogies of the great-heartedness of Nicholas II and the heights of his political genius! And what a bitter disappointment to France! People will naturally say that we hoped the Russian alliance would serve as a lever against Germany, a means of sooner or later recovering our lost provinces; and now this alliance, for which we sacrificed so much, is to serve only to mask a *rapprochement* between Russia and the German powers!"

After delivering himself of this explosive speech, he calmed down and went on:

"What am I to do in this situation? Your chief, Nisard, has given me an idea which I believe to be sound, and even very ingenious: namely, that we should deprive the Russian project of all political significance by diverting it into the field of academic debate, the discussion of problems of pure law and theoretical jurisprudence. Isn't that ingenious? But for that task, which I wish to carry out myself, I need you and your files, because I want to have at my finger tips the whole story of the negotiation of the alliance from the very outset."

I immediately fetched my files and explained to the Minister the spirit in which the treaty was negotiated and finally concluded, the objects of the negotiators, and the accompanying written, verbal, or tacit agreements.

When I had finished, Delcassé said:

"I should like you to discuss all this with General de Boisdeffre. The signatory of the military convention should at least be kept informed of our ideas; and he might be able to give us good advice."

"He not only might be able to give us good advice, but also might be able to write personally to General Kuropatkin, the Minister of War, with whom he is very friendly, in the spirit of your ideas; and no one is in a better position than Kuropatkin to defend them in the presence of the Czar."

"Go and see Boisdeffre for me."

"Of course!"

I presented myself at the office of the Chief of the General Staff at about six o'clock. The porter, though he knows me well, said to me in an embarrassed manner, as if he were showing out an importunate caller:

"Yes, General de Boisdeffre is in Paris. . . . He has just arrived from the country. . . . He doesn't want to see anybody. . . . I think he is with the Minister. . . . You would do better not to wait, sir!"

I next went to see General Gonse. The porter behaved in the same evasive fashion.

Finally I fell back on the intelligence department, with whom I had some business to settle. The office messenger, who looked strange, said to me:

"Lieutenant-Colonel Henry is on leave; I don't know when he's coming back. . . . Captain Junck is away; I

don't know when he's coming back either. . . . None of
the gentlemen are here.''

"Then why are you here?''

He muttered something unintelligible. I went away,
wondering.

This evening, on the club terrace, I had a long conversation with Eugène-Melchior de Vogüé who, because of his Russian connections, is very upset by
Nicholas II's rescript.

"What! The Emperor did not consult us before
launching such a program on the world!'' he exclaimed.
"It's unbelievable! It's monstrous! The alliance will
never survive it! And to say that if old Bismarck had
lived only thirty days longer [23] he would have lived to
see this! Can't you imagine the flash in his dying
eyes?''

Vogüé attributed to Pobedonostsev a vital role in the
working out of the astonishing manifesto; he did not
doubt that the whole thing had been secretly handled
by the intrepid champion of Orthodox autocracy.

From Pobedonostsev "the Russian Torquemada,'' it
was an easy step to Cavaignac, whom we had often
used to meet at the Taine receptions, and this was the
character we drew of him: a harsh, surly man, possessed of virtuous ambition and a touchy pride, coldly
passionate, inexorable in his resentments, intransigent
in his beliefs, a powerful dialectician, incisive in
speech; he could easily be imagined in the role of Grand
Inquisitor.

[23] Bismarck had died at Friedrichsruhe on July 31, 1898.

Tuesday, August 30, 1898

This evening the final bulletin of the Havas agency included the following:

Today, in the office of the Minister of War, Lieutenant-Colonel Henry was identified as and admitted himself to be the author of the letter, dated October, 1896, in which Dreyfus is named. The Minister of War immediately ordered the arrest of Lieutenant-Colonel Henry, who was taken to the Fortress of Mont-Valérien.

Why Mont Valérien? The crime of which Henry "admitted himself" to be guilty is, after all, something very different from an infraction of discipline; it is a crime in common law, the forgery of a public document. So why was the forger not sent straight to the Cherche-Midi prison?

Wednesday, August 31, 1898

The President of the Republic this afternoon signed a decree by which Esterhazy is "cashiered for habitual misconduct." The court of inquiry formed to pronounce judgment on him threw out the charge of dishonorable conduct. So the uhlan remains a man of honor in the eyes of his peers!

Thursday, September 1, 1898

Lieutenant-Colonel Henry cut his throat with his razor between three and four o'clock yesterday afternoon in the room in which he was confined alone, without the slightest surveillance, at Mont-Valérien.

The Minister sent for me this morning as soon as I arrived at the Quai d'Orsay. He was striding up and down his office.

"Well!" he said. "Now the fat is in the fire! What do you conclude from these events?"

"I conclude that the case will have to be reopened immediately."

After a silence, Delcassé said:

"Do you believe there are other forgeries in the Dreyfus file?"

"I should not be surprised if there were another two or three, at least. But that is only suspicion. I am thinking of certain documents that Henry spoke to me mysteriously about several times, but was never willing to show me."

Delcassé then told me some details about the strange circumstances in which a young officer attached to Cavaignac's private office, Captain Cuignet, had discovered that the letter attributed to Panizzardi was a forgery.[24]

"Would you believe," he went on, "that the Minister of War kept this discovery to himself for a fortnight? He did not even inform the Prime Minister. Can you explain such silence in such a grave matter?"

[24] Louis Cuignet, born 1857, entered Saint-Cyr in 1878, was promoted captain in 1890. In July, 1896, Cavaignac, the Minister of War, made him his aide-de-camp. Cuignet's discovery of the forgery committed by Henry did not, however, cause him to rally to the side of those who believed in Dreyfus' innocence. He was promoted major in 1899 and put on the retired list in 1906.

"No, I cannot. But how does M. Cavaignac explain it?"

"He claims that before informing the Council of Ministers he wanted to submit the document to a series of expert checks and counter-checks."

"What a joke! Six months have passed since the Foreign Ministry informed the Ministry of War of an official declaration by the Italian Government that if the Dreyfus file contained any document whatever implying that there had been relations of any kind between Dreyfus and Panizzardi, that document was apocryphal. I have myself repeated that to General de Boisdeffre, General Gonse, and Lieutenant-Colonel Henry again and again. In any case, quite apart from the positive evidence that brought the forgery to light, of which I know nothing, the text of the document stinks of forgery by itself. . . . I've got to the point of wondering whether the fortnight during which M. Cavaignac kept the terrible secret to himself was not used to expurgate the secret file and eliminate some too strikingly obvious forgeries, the Kaiser's letters, for example."

"It's fantastic! . . . As for a reopening of the case, I believe, as you do, that it is as necessary as it is inevitable. But Cavaignac is more opposed to it than ever. He says that Dreyfus' guilt is as clear to him as it ever was."

In conclusion, Delcassé told me that General de Boisdeffre had at his own request been relieved of his post and had been succeeded by General Renouard, the commandant of the École de Guerre.

Panizzardi has been appointed colonel of the 5th Regiment of Bersaglieri and has just left Paris.

Monday, September 5, 1898

I called at the intelligence department for the first time since the drama. I found there Captain Junck, Captain Mareschal, and the archivist Gribelin. Consternation and dismay were written on their faces. "It's a catastrophe! An ineradicable stain on the honor of the army! Worse than Sedan!" They assured me, their eyes shining with tears, that nobody in the service had suspected the forgery. In any case, the document had been seized immediately by General Gonse. Finally, Lieutenant-Colonel Henry had inspired absolute confidence in all his colleagues. "We liked him so much. Even when he spoke sharply to us, as he often did, we felt him to be so honest, so devoted, so good!" Gribelin, who was sobbing, said:

"M. Paléologue, you, who knew him so well, do not doubt that he was a good man?"

"Alas! I can no longer believe it."

I managed to bring the conversation round to the origin and fabrication of the apocryphal document. According to Gribelin, it must have been faked at the end of October, 1896. Henry's object had been to counter the uneasiness caused in the minds of Billot, Boisdeffre, and Gonse by Picquart's "maneuvers." I said to Gribelin:

"When the document was introduced into your files, Major Lauth must have seen it. How is it that he didn't detect the forgery?"

"He was on thirty days' leave when the document was forged; he first saw it five or six months later, when General Gonse gave it to him to be photographed."

"He photographed it? Then he must have looked at it closely, held it in his hands, had the opportunity to examine it at leisure. How is it that he didn't suspect a fake, an imposture?"

"I don't know. Major Lauth always believed it to be a genuine document, just as we did."

"But Major Lauth is shrewd, even very shrewd. He has had years of experience of examining handwriting and checking suspicious documents, and in matters of this kind I have always found him unusually acute. I cannot believe that a document so important, and written in such a strange style as the faked Panizzardi letter, did not rouse his suspicions. I cannot believe that the idea never passed through his head that Henry might have been taken in by one of your doubtful agents, Leeman or Lajoux, or somebody of the sort."

Gribelin, very embarrassed, replied:

"Major Lauth, with whom I went to Mont-Valérien to watch Lieutenant-Colonel Henry's body, assured me that he never had the slightest suspicion about the genuineness of the document." [25]

[25] The text of the letter forged by Henry was:

My Dear Friend,

I have read that a deputy is going to make an interpellation about Dreyfus. If new explanations are asked for in Rome, I shall say that I never had relations with this Jew. That is understood. If you are asked, say the same, because nobody must ever know what took place with him.

ALEXANDRINE

Tuesday, September 6, 1898

Thinking over my conversation with the archivist Gribelin yesterday, I find one more argument in favor of my inference that a vital role in the shady secret history of the Dreyfus case is to be attributed to Major Lauth.

As long ago as 1894, I noticed that Henry and Lauth were on terms of intimacy far exceeding those of service comradeship. Even outside the office, they saw a great deal of each other. How often have I seen them together, returning on horseback from a morning outing in the Bois! The two men differed so much that their close friendship struck me as odd. Henry was a big, rough peasant, of only rudimentary education and limited intelligence, as common in his language as in his manners; Lauth, a handsome, distinguished-looking, meticulously dressed, unapproachable-looking cavalry officer, with a quick and ready mind. I found it hard to imagine what held the two men together.

The explanation was given to me in 1896 by Lieu-

To forge this document Henry used two insignificant letters written to Schwartzkoppen by Panizzardi ("Alexandrine"). He skillfully combined phrases from both and added some words referring to Dreyfus made up by himself. For this purpose he made use of one of his agents, Moïse Leeman, known as Lemercier-Picard, a man with ten convictions for fraud. The two accomplices failed to notice that, though both letters were written on squared paper, the squares on each were not identical; in one case the lines were blue and in the other violet. On March 3, 1898, thirteen days after Henry's faked letter was quoted at Zola's trial by General de Pellieux, Lemercier-Picard was found hanged from the fastening of a Paris hotel bedroom window; the circumstances of his death were never cleared up.

tenant-Colonel Cordier, when he came to say good-by
to me on leaving the intelligence department.[26] In
Sandherr's time Cordier and I had handled a number
of very delicate matters together, with the result that
we had learned to trust and be very frank with each
other. Thus he had had no hesitation in saying to me:
"Be on your guard against Henry and Lauth, or
rather be on your guard against Lauth, for it is he who
holds the leading strings." When I expressed astonishment that an elderly major should allow himself to be
led by a young captain, Cordier told me that Lauth
had a hold over Henry through Henry's wife, whose
lover he was. This caused more surprise on my part;
never having seen Mme Henry, I imagined her as re-
sembling her husband, that is to say, bulky, mature,
and middle-aged. But Cordier went on as follows:
"Mme Henry," he said, "comes from Péronne, where
Henry was town major in 1892. Her father, one Bertin-
court, kept a hostelry for wagoners there; his daughter helped him to serve the customers. She was pretty
and attractive, with a beautiful complexion. Henry
noticed her, and she kept him dangling so skillfully that
he ended by marrying her. A few months later, under
the patronage of Boisdeffre, who proposed to use him
as his personal spy, Henry was posted to the intelli-

[26] Albert Cordier, born 1844, left Saint-Cyr in 1866 and fought
in the 1870 war as an infantry lieutenant. He was promoted captain
in 1885, became an instructor at the École de Guerre, and was deputy
chief of the intelligence department from 1892 to 1896, with the rank
of major and later of lieutenant-colonel. He was removed from the
active list because of temporary disability in September, 1896, and
retired in June, 1899.

gence department. His wife used to call on him there. One day, when he was out, Lauth, as if by chance, received her in his office. Now ill chance had it that the door was suddenly opened by our fierce and faithful watchdog, the old Algerian rifleman Bachir, and his Muslim modesty was shocked by what he saw. He immediately came to see me and denounced the guilty couple, and I had a lot of trouble in calming him down. . . . Since then the gallant adventure has turned into a liaison. Does Henry suspect that he is being cuckolded? Does he prefer not to notice it? I have no idea. In any case, he is absolutely dominated by Lauth, who handles him like a puppet."

Once, in spring last year, I met Henry, Mme Henry, and Lauth on the Esplanade des Invalides. At once I understood everything. Mme Henry is tall, slender, dark, with pretty features and beautiful bright eyes. True, she dresses in a rather provincial style, but the freshness of her twenty-five years and the suppleness of her figure make her very attractive.

Thus I have started wondering whether Lauth could have been ignorant of a single one of the criminal maneuvers that drove Henry to suicide; and if he was aware of them, why he should have covered them, even lent his hand to them? I go further. In this obscure drama cannot the instigation and the initiative nearly always be traced back to Lauth? But what personal interest could he have had that was powerful enough to make him have an innocent man convicted and then kept in jail by the most abominable means, *per fas et nefas?* Perhaps I should not have asked this question if I had not for some time past had an idea that would greatly change the whole aspect of the Dreyfus case by linking the act of treason of 1894 with a series of similar, mysterious events on which no light has yet been cast which started to occur about 1886 and went on until 1896, without Dreyfus' being in any way involved.

Cavaignac last night resigned as Minister of War; his successor is General Zurlinden, the Military Governor of Paris.[27]

Monday, September 26, 1898

For the past fortnight the humiliating Fashoda affair has given me only too many opportunities of working directly with the Minister, because he wanted either to refer to the files on the Russian alliance or to make use of my normal relations with the naval staff.

In the Fashoda affair the French public, alarmed as it is by the threatening attitude adopted by Britain, does not realize the poverty, the hopeless inadequacy, of our naval resources. There is not a single point along our coast, from Dunkirk to Bayonne, from Port-Vendres to Nice, from Bonifacio to Bastia, from Oran to Bizerte, that is capable of resisting an attack by the British Fleet; and at Guadeloupe, Dakar, Jibouti, Diégo-Suarez, and Tonkin matters are still worse. I

[27] General Zurlinden (1837–1929) had been War Minister once before, in the Ribot Cabinet of 1895. Brisson appointed him to succeed Cavaignac on September 6, 1898, but he resigned twelve days later, being unwilling to dissociate himself from his predecessors, whose belief in Dreyfus' guilt he shared.

remember that last May Post Captain Boué de Lapey-
rère, who once took me to Korea in "La Vipère" and
was going to assume command of the Newfoundland
station, said to me: "For heaven's sake, don't go to
war with Britain! It would be more shameful and more
irreparable than Sedan!" And at about the same time
Admiral Sallandrouze de la Mornaix confessed to me
that the brilliant facade of our naval power was
nothing but a sham.

The terrible way in which France is rent by the
Dreyfus crisis, which for some weeks has reached a
state of paroxysm, greatly aggravates the difficulties,
not to say the dangers, of the external situation.

Delcassé has, therefore, been vigorously applying
himself to removing the Dreyfus case from the political
field in order to confine it to the judicial field; he hopes
that the sheer slowness, methodicalness, complication,
and unintelligibility of legal procedure will end by
blunting the sharp edge of the irritant provided by the
hateful case.

Thus, at the Cabinet meeting that was held this
morning at the Place Beauvau on the question of reopening the case, the Foreign Minister fought with all
his strength the opposition of the majority of his colleagues to a reconsideration of the 1894 verdict. He
gained his point by six votes to four.[28] The Cour de
Cassation will be apprised of the matter tomorrow.

[28] The consultative committee of appeal, which had met previously,
had recommended the opposite, on the ground that the Henry
forgery was an event subsequent to the 1894 court-martial and had,
therefore, not been a material factor leading to the conviction; in
its eyes it was therefore not a "new fact" of a nature justifying a
reopening of the case. But the 1896 forgery made all the other docu-

It is expected that hearings will begin in the Criminal
Chamber of the Cour de Cassation in a month.

Monday, October 31, 1898

The Brisson Ministry, much weakened by internal dissensions and the debates in the Chamber, has had to
resign. It has been succeeded by a Cabinet formed by
Charles Dupuy.[29] Delcassé retains the portfolio of Foreign Affairs, and Freycinet becomes Minister of War.[30]

Thursday, November 3, 1898

The Fashoda humiliation is now complete. The French
Government has been forced to bow to the arrogance
and inflexibility of the British Cabinet. The Marchand
mission has received orders to abandon its camp on the
Upper Nile and return to France by way of Abyssinia.

After a plea by Manau, the Procurator-General, and
a report by Bard, the judge of appeal, both in favor of
quashing the 1894 verdict, the Criminal Chamber has
just begun an inquiry into the Dreyfus case.

---

ments suspect, and the Government, having the final power of decision, overruled the committee.

[29] This was the third Dupuy Cabinet (November 4, 1898-June 12,
1899).

[30] There had been five holders of this thorny office since the beginning of the Dreyfus case. Dupuy's object in calling on Freycinet
was to entrust it to a personality of the first rank. Charles de Saulces
de Freycinet (1828–1923), a mining engineer, had in 1870 been
Gambetta's principal colleague in the organization of national defense. He had been a life senator since 1876, had been Prime Minister four times (1879–1880, 1882, 1886, 1890–92), and Minister of
War without interruption for five years (1888–93).

Tuesday, November 15, 1898

Since the eighth of this month, the Criminal Chamber
has been conducting its inquiry into the Dreyfus case
in camera.

General Mercier, General Billot, Cavaignac, General
Zurlinden, and General Chanoine have already appeared before it. But their evidence, which was obviously concerted, has brought nothing new to light because on every obscure point they refused to answer,
taking refuge behind reasons of state.

To find a way out of the blind alley in which it finds
itself, the Criminal Chamber has asked for the secret
file kept by the intelligence department.

Thursday, November 17, 1898

The Queen Regent of Spain has just conferred on
the President of the Republic the Order of the Golden
Fleece.

The ceremony of bestowing the insignia was carried
out this afternoon at the Élysée palace by Queen Maria
Christina's delegates, Señor Montero-Rios, the
Marqués de Villalobar and the Marqués de Novella, in
the presence of the Ambassador, Señor León y Castillo.
The Grand Duke Vladimir Alexandrovich acted as
Félix Faure's sponsor.

This evening there was a dinner followed by a gala
reception in the sumptuous surroundings of the Élysée.
The setting was magnificent and in perfect taste.

At dinner the President of the Republic sat in state

between the Grand Duchess Maria Pavlovna and Señora Léon y Castillo. Opposite him his modest wife, looking resigned, was enthroned between the Grand Duke Vladimir [31] and the Grand Duke Alexis.[32]

From the point of display, everything was for the best. But at the mere sight of the program, I could not help a feeling of dismay. Was not this coupling of the French and Spanish flags symbolic? Are we not on the slope that led Spain to its irreparable decline? Shall we not in our turn go through an era of long internal dissension and a humiliating era of men like Serrano, Narvaez, Prim, and Espartero?

Toward the end of the evening, I talked to the Grand Duke Vladimir, whom I have met several times recently at the Comtesse de Perchenstein's and at the Comtesse de Talleyrand's. In the tone of brusque frankness that is customary with him, he said to me:

"I congratulate you on serving under M. Delcassé. He has courage, patriotism, skill. We have had a thorough discussion of the alliance, and I have seen that he understands it well; he is actually the first of your Ministers who has understood it so well. May God grant that he remain in power for some time! In that

[31] The Grand Duke Vladimir Alexandrovich (1847–1909) was the second son of Alexander II. He married Maria Pavlovna, Duchess of Mecklenburg.

[32] Grand Duke Alexis Alexandrovich (1850–1908) was the third son of Alexander II. He was the Admiral General, "supreme chief of the Fleet and of the Naval Administration," and a member of the Imperial Council. In 1905 Russian opinion attributed to him the principal responsibility for the defeats inflicted on the Russian navy by the Japanese.

case I warrant you that France will have a fine position in Europe!''

The idea that the mysterious file of that holy tabernacle, the intelligence department, may be disclosed to the Criminal Chamber has once more caused the Nationalists to rage. ''What?'' they say. ''Is the Government thus to deliver up all the secrets of our national defense to a pack of false and traitorous judges? Does the Government not know that the disclosure of certain documents would mean war with Germany?''

There is great excitement in the lobbies of the Palais Bourbon.

Delcassé sent for me to ask me, on the Prime Minister's behalf, if I thought that submission to the court of the secret file ''and the indiscretions that might result'' might not risk putting us in an awkward position in relation to Germany. I replied:

''The question that is worrying the Prime Minister is not peculiar to the Dreyfus case; it has already arisen in many espionage trials. Now, a few very simple precautions are sufficient to safeguard the diplomatic proprieties. None of these trials has ever created the slightest difficulty with Germany. And what if Germany did complain? We should have our reply. France has not yet declined to the rank of Honduras or Nicaragua. There is, however, a point that I wish to bring to your notice. Is not the intelligence department, in which the spirit of the past is still very much alive,

holding in reserve a number of ultra-secret documents
to be produced as a last resort? I refer, for instance,
to the notes or letters attributed to the Kaiser. These
are the documents to which Henry referred when he
spoke of a 'bludgeon-stroke,' the documents that
Esterhazy picturesquely called 'the imperial guard.'
I have some reason to believe that after Henry's suicide those notes or letters were destroyed, but I cannot
guarantee it. In any case, if they still exist, from the
diplomatic point of view their disclosure would be
completely harmless; the only disadvantage would be
that we should be discredited in the eyes of Europe because the result would be a huge roar of laughter."

Delcassé accepted what I said.

Wednesday, November 23, 1898

One of the strangest psychological symptoms I have
observed in the course of the moral crisis through
which France is passing, which in so many respects
resembles a religious crisis, is the storm of anger
roused among the Nationalists by the possibility of
the disclosure of the secret file.

For months and months they have been repeating
that the General Staff secret file is bursting with evidence against Dreyfus, some of it so unheard-of, so
decisive, so shattering, that if it were made known the
whole Jewish race would be transfixed. Now they regard the mere possibility of such a disclosure as an
abominable sacrilege.

In the same way no devotee of St. Januarius at

Naples would agree to the exposure of the mysterious phial to the curiosity of the profane.

In the domain of faith, evidence is effective only if it is intangible. *Noli me tangere!*

Friday, November 25, 1898

After listening for four days to the detailed and methodical evidence of General Roget,[33] the Criminal Chamber has ordered the appearance of Lieutenant-Colonel Picquart, who has spent one hundred and twenty-five days in the Cherche-Midi prison waiting to be court-martialed for "forgery."

Picquart was therefore brought to the Palais de Justice under the escort of a captain of *gendarmerie.*

Monday, November 28, 1898

The proceedings being instituted against Lieutenant-Colonel Picquart and the simultaneous, continuous stream of appalling insults being poured on the judges of the Criminal Chamber by the Nationalist press have led to a violent debate in the Palais Bourbon.

To everybody's surprise, Poincaré spoke. Having been a Minister in 1894 at the time of Dreyfus' conviction, for the past two years he had prudently avoided intervening in the battle. His appearance on the rostrum was, therefore, all the more significant. With his very first words, he attacked. "This time it is enough!"

[33] General Roget, former principal private secretary to Cavaignac at the Ministry of War, was one of the most ardent believers in Dreyfus' guilt.

he said. "My silence at the present hour would be an
act of cowardice." He went on to stigmatize the "intolerable abuses" discovered in certain offices of the
General Staff and the "disgraceful maneuvers" by
which attempts were still being made to prevent their
full disclosure. "If it is true that a judicial error was
made in 1894, it is the imperious duty of those of us who
were then in the Government to do nothing that might
prevent its reparation." A deputy of the Right called
out: "Why didn't you speak sooner?" His reply was
skillful. "I foresaw that objection," he said. "If I did
not speak sooner, it was because the competent judicial
authority was not yet charged with the matter. But
now the time has come when all who know a fragment
of the truth must declare it. I know well that in breaking the silence that has been weighing on me, I am ex-
posing myself to attacks, insults, slanders. What does
it matter? I am happy at having at last liberated my
conscience."

This firm language, of which Freycinet, the War
Minister, and Charles Dupuy, the Prime Minister, skillfully took advantage, assured the Government of a big
majority. The Criminal Chamber will thus be able to
go on with its work—until the next incident.

Tuesday, December 20, 1898

General de Galliffet,[34] General Gonse, and General de

[34] Gaston, Marquis de Galliffet (1830–1909), volunteered for the
cavalry in 1848 and gained all his promotions on the battlefield, in
the Crimea, Africa, Italy, and Mexico. In 1870, as a brigadier-
general, he led the famous cavalry charge at Sedan. He came over

Boisdeffre have given evidence at length in the Criminal Chamber during the past few days.

At the Palais Bourbon yesterday the fiery Nationalist deputy Lasies interpellated the Minister of War in a last effort to prevent the secret file from being submitted to the Cour de Cassation. After a debate that was as confused as it was lively, the submission of the file to the court was agreed to in principle, subject to acceptance by the court of all the security measures required by the Government.

Friday, December 23, 1898

The German press publishes this unofficial statement:

The declarations of the Imperial Government have made it clear that no German personality, high or low, has had dealings of any kind with Dreyfus. On the German side there can be no objection to the publication of the secret file in full.

Moreover, we do not believe French statesmen to be so ill-advised as seriously to believe that this file contains letters or notes from his Majesty the Emperor having any connection with the Dreyfus case. Only those capable of believing such insanities would have anything to fear from a complete disclosure.

---

early to the Republic, was singled out by Gambetta, and had a brilliant career. In June, 1899, Waldeck-Rousseau appointed him War Minister in his "Government of national defense." He resigned on May 28, 1900, and was succeeded by General André.

Saturday, December 24, 1898

General de Gonse has just called on me at home in the Boulevard Malesherbes to talk to me "in a friendly and private manner" about the famous Panizzardi telegram.

When I had finished giving him the most detailed particulars about its deciphering, he said:

"Why wouldn't you give Henry a copy when he came and asked you for it on my behalf last spring?"

"Because it is an absolute rule at the Quai d'Orsay that a secret document may not be given to anyone personally. I explained to Henry that I was perfectly prepared to give him an authenticated copy if he produced an official request for it in writing. Meanwhile, I dictated the text of the telegram to him verbatim, and he copied it out."

This took the general aback. He gazed at me with astonishment written in his big, lack-luster eyes, and muttered:

"But . . . but . . . that wasn't the story Henry told me at all! All he said was that you had refused to give him the telegram and had not been friendly to him. . . . I then reported to General Billot, who told me to ask the Post Office for the document. I went to them and asked for the original of the telegram, but was told that they no longer had it, that it had been destroyed."

"In the first place, why did you not follow the official, regular procedure, that is to say, why did you not make a proper application in writing? And, in the second place, you should not have asked for the original, for the originals of all telegrams whatsoever are burned within eighteen months. You should have asked for one of the tracings of the original, because the tracings are preserved indefinitely.''

''True, I insisted on having the original. . . . But they might have told me what you have just told me. . . . But I didn't quite understand what you've just been saying. . . .''

The poor man's entanglement in his own stupidity is pitiable to behold.

I conclude from this conversation, however, that in April, 1898, Lieutenant-Colonel Henry made yet another attempt to suppress the telegram of November 2, 1894, which was so favorable to Dreyfus.

Thursday, December 29, 1898

Delcassé sent for me at about three o'clock this afternoon and asked me to bring him the diplomatic file on the Dreyfus case.

I found him in conference with the Prime Minister, Charles Dupuy, an old politician, a solidly built man with a clear, subtle, and wily mind.

Scarcely had I exhibited a few documents from my file when Dupuy interrupted me. His eyes were shining, and there was a look of wonderment in his eyes, as if I had suddenly opened up before him a whole new horizon that he had never suspected, as if he had suddenly seen all the pawns and pieces laid out for a political maneuver.

"What you are showing me is of vital importance," he exclaimed. "It's the very crux of the whole case!"

After that he did not interrupt again; I could tell that he had made up his mind. When I had finished he said:

"The Cour de Cassation must take cognizance of this file. You will submit it to them. . . . Don't you agree, Delcassé?"

But Delcassé did not seem to me to be enthusiastic about this idea. He asked me what I thought. My opinion was clear.

"I don't think we can avoid submitting it to the court. Sooner or later, we shall be asked for it. Let us not wait to produce it until we are forced. In any case our file is irreproachable. Certainly, some precautions would have to be taken to preserve the diplomatic proprieties."

"Of course!" Delcassé said. "Write out your own instructions. I shall sign them with my eyes shut."

Meanwhile Charles Dupuy had risen to his feet. With his hands behind his back and his head sunk between his shoulders, he was pacing heavily up and down, without saying anything. Then he stopped and rested his hands on a table as if he were at the rostrum, and made us the following speech:

"This file which you have just read me is the salvation of Dreyfus. Have no doubt of it! But, when we have saved Dreyfus, how shall we save the army? The generals themselves must admit their mistake, for it is only round them that the army will rally. General Mercier, General de Boisdeffre, and General Gonse, their eyes opened by your file, must appear before the Criminal Chamber and boldly announce that they have been mistaken. The army will believe them, and only them. Is such a sacrifice too much to expect of their courage and their patriotism? I shall not insult them by doubting it. If on the battlefield they received the order: 'Charge! Go and get yourself killed for the safety of the army!'—do you imagine that they would hesitate for a single moment? Why, then, should they refuse to march today?"

After this rhetorical effusion, the practical man suddenly reasserted himself.

"I was wrong to mention General Mercier," he went on. "With him there's nothing to be done. His mind is hypnotized. For him Dreyfus' guilt is a transcendent syllogism, an indestructible dogma. But, you who know them well, do you not think that I could convert General de Boisdeffre and General Gonse?"

"Convert them?" I replied. "Oh, no! Mr. Prime Minister, do not count on that! I have known General de Boisdeffre for nearly twenty years. The Russian alliance has often caused me to have a great deal to do with him and, in spite of the difference in our ages, we have a number of friends in common. Well! everything that I know about him, his character, his beliefs, his environment, his whole past life, prevents me from believing that he will fall in with your idea. Henry's suicide was a terrible blow to him; it broke him morally. Since then he has shut himself up in the country, in silence, prayer, and poverty. If tomorrow I were told that he had become a Carthusian or a Trappist, I should not be in the least surprised. But I cannot see him walking up the steps of the Palais de Justice in full uniform with decorations to make a solemn recantation in favor of Dreyfus before a civilian court. . . . As for General Gonse, he is dimmer, duller, more limited in intelligence than ever. I saw him last Saturday and he is a rag. . . . In conclusion, Mr. Prime Minister, there is a point to which I take the liberty of drawing your attention. The Dreyfus case is no longer in the political field; it is now *sub judice.* Do you not fear that any intervention on your part with General de Boisdeffre and General Gonse might be considered an attempt to bring pressure to bear on them with a view to influencing their evidence?''

Charles Dupuy's face suddenly darkened.

''You are right; I give up the idea,'' he said. ''But I shall see you again soon. Before you appear before the Criminal Chamber, I wish to see your instructions.''

Thereupon he took his departure. Delcassé asked me to remain.

''I see that you have understood me well,'' he said. ''Henceforward the Dreyfus case must be confined to the judicial sphere. In any case, I do not wish it to hamper my political action. I did not come to the Quai d'Orsay to remain inactive; I have a heavy task to perform, and I intend to carry it out to good purpose.''

Then he started talking to me about his negotiations with Britain, which were going well; soon the evacuation of Fashoda will be no more than a sad memory. He also said that he was delighted with his relations with Muraviev.

In this connection I told him that the Grand Duke Vladimir had recently said to me at dinner at the Comtesse de Talleyrand's: "I hope to live long enough to hear England's death-rattle. That is the ardent prayer that I address to God each day!"

Delcassé started, his face aghast.

"What a mistake, what blindness!" he declared. "For Russia as for France, England is a rival, a competitor, and her behavior is often very, very unpleasant, very harsh. But she is not an enemy, and above all she is not *the* enemy. . . . Ah! my dear Paléologue, if only Russia, Britain, and France could ally themselves against Germany!"

4. THE COUR DE CASSATION

4. THE COUR DE CASSATION

Another visit from General Gonse, to whom I explained and demonstrated for the hundredth time the true translation of the Panizzardi telegram!!! But nothing can penetrate that poor, confused brain.

Then, seeing him utterly downcast and feeling that he wanted to unburden himself, I explained to him how, after so firmly believing in Dreyfus' guilt, I had come round to be convinced of his innocence. He interrupted me several times. "It's terrifying!" he said. "It's crazy!" . . . "I don't understand!" . . . "I didn't notice!" On the crux of the matter, he avoided committing himself, but when he got up to go he remained for some moments with his nose glued to the windowpane, absorbed in a brown study, gazing at the rainy spectacle of the Boulevard Malesherbes; then, with his eyes suddenly full of tears, he said to me:

"In short, I am either the worst of wretches or the worst of fools!"

A painful dilemma. I comforted the poor general as well as I could.

Tuesday, January 3, 1899

I now think I am able to formulate a constructive hypothesis to explain the origin and background of the Dreyfus case. It is as follows:

The act of treason that supplied the motive for securing Dreyfus' conviction in 1894 is associated with a chain of similar events that began in 1886 and continued to 1896.

These events are attributable to three persons, who worked sometimes in conjunction, sometimes separately, and, in this last case, without each other's knowledge.

The German, Austrian, and Italian General Staffs for whom these three individuals worked seem to have had direct contact with only two of them; they may even not have known the name of the third, who, however, was the member of the trio best able to provide them with valuable information. The first is Maurice Weil; the second is Major Esterhazy; the third, on whom no suspicion yet rests, is an officer of very high rank who, after holding important office in the War Ministry for several years, is now in command of troops.

Lieutenant-Colonel Henry had an interest in covering Esterhazy, whose friend and debtor he had been. Major Lauth had different motives—motives of a private nature—for covering the third traitor. That is why from the very beginning of the Dreyfus case, the arrival of the *bordereau*, the connivance of Henry and Lauth was immediate and complete, and they had no need for a moment to put their heads together. Their immediate connivance was necessary in order to cause it to be believed that the *bordereau* had been picked up in pieces in a wastepaper basket in the German Embassy, while in reality it had been abstracted, intact and still in its envelope, from the porter's lodge at the Embassy. If Henry and Lauth had been alone at that moment, no doubt they would have destroyed it; but at that moment Captain Matton came in and saw it in theirs hands.[1] It was thus impossible to suppress the document, and there was no way of avoiding the investigation which was immediately ordered by Sandherr. Now, in the course of this investigation a certain resemblance was noted between the handwriting of the *bordereau* and that of Dreyfus who, by an additional ill chance, was a Jew. . . . Henceforward, throughout the preliminaries and the judicial proceedings, the fraudulent practices of Henry and Lauth did not cease. They started again with the same audacious spon-

[1] Pierre Matton, born 1856, was an artillery officer. He was promoted to captain in 1884 and was in the intelligence department from 1893 to 1898, when he was given his majority and became military attaché in the French Embassy at St. Petersburg. He was promoted to brigadier-general in 1913 and was put on the reserve in 1915.

taneity when Colonel Picquart began making inquiries about Esterhazy in April, 1896.

In the light of this hypothesis, what terrible clarity and significance attaches to the phrase from the letter that Henry wrote to his wife a few minutes before he cut his throat: "You know in *whose* interest I acted"!

Friday, January 6, 1899

I went with Delcassé to the Ministry of the Interior in the Place Beauvau to submit to the Prime Minister the instructions to which I shall have to conform before the Cour de Cassation.

Charles Dupuy unreservedly approved my draft. He then told us about a number of more or less scandalous incidents that had just occurred in the precincts of the Criminal Chamber and demonstrated that public passions had invaded the court.

"You will find a feverish atmosphere there," he said. "I count on your prudence and coolness."

Saturday, January 7, 1899

I am to appear before the Criminal Chamber the day after tomorrow.

The chief clerk of the court has unofficially informed me that my examination will bear on the whole of the Dreyfus case, that it will be pretty long—two or three hours, perhaps—and that I shall be well advised to refresh my memory beforehand, because I shall not be allowed to use any notes.

The Criminal Chamber consists of a presiding judge,

thirteen other judges, and an advocate-general. Loew, the president, a typical old-style judge who enjoys universal respect, belongs to an austere Alsatian bourgeois family. In the *Libre Parole* this has earned him the epithet of "Prussian."

Monday, January 9, 1899

I reached the Palais de Justice shortly before midday; the sky was pallid and snowy.

Mounting the steps that lead to the Cour de Cassation, I reflected that the "temple of the law" that I was entering had, in the Nationalist press, become the "sanctuary of treason," "a branch of the synagogue," "the lair of Judas," "a combination of Bourse and brothel." It was here that "every day, throughout the twenty-four hours, the Kaiser receives the most secret information about our war plans and our national defense." I, therefore, knew what to expect as soon as my evidence became known.

While midday was striking, an usher asked me to follow him.

The Criminal Chamber sits in an oblong hall which backs on to the Galérie de St. Louis, and it is sadly lighted from the interior Cour du Dépot. At one end the president's bench forms a kind of rostrum. The judges' benches are each on a dais to right and left. At the other end is the desk of the clerk of the court, and in the center a witness' chair. All the judges were in black robes.

After the usual formalities, which were supplemented by the reading of my instructions, President

Loew examined me about the beginnings of the Dreyfus case.[2]

Questions were put to me in the most courteous manner, with a system, a precision, and an impartiality
which impressed me. I was made to explain one by one
the various documents or pieces of information that
it had been my duty to bring to the notice of the War
Ministry, to describe my personal relations with General de Boisdeffre, General Gonse, Colonel Sandherr,
and Lieutenant-Colonel Henry, and to recapitulate all
that the Foreign Ministry had been able to find out
about the treasonable events that had led to the 1894
trial.

In the course of the discussion, which was at times
very animated, one of the judges, taking up one of my
statements, asked me what "consequences" I drew
from it and to what "explanation" and "hypotheses"
it led me. I categorically declined to reply, for the role
of a witness is not to offer his personal appreciations
and conjectures, but to state what he has seen, what
he knows, and nothing else.

Another judge trenchantly expressed approval of
what I had said. There was discussion and argument on
all the benches. President Loew re-established silence
by saying to me, with a smile:

"It is you, sir, who are legally in the right."

[2] *Author's note:* The official text of my evidence as established by
the clerk of the court but not containing "elements of discussion exchanged outside the record of evidence," was published in *la Révi-
sion du procès Dreyfus, enquête de la Cour de cassation,* 2 vols.,
Paris, 1899.

The court adjourned twice to allow me a few minutes' rest. No sooner had I reached the doorway than
a loud buzz of voices arose behind me.

During the second adjournment, which I spent in an
office from which the whole vast and noble panorama of
the Seine was visible, the clerk came and offered me,
on behalf of the president of the court, a cup of tea
which I eagerly accepted. In return I offered him a
cigarette, which he similarly accepted. Then, with an
air of secrecy, he said:

"We have time for a smoke. . . . You have told us
such interesting and unexpected things, sir, that the
Chamber is quite moved. Your evidence is the first
since the proceedings began that has given us objec-
tive and conclusive information; you will have noticed
with what attention the gentlemen have been listening
to you. They are exchanging their ideas at this moment
and, as you can guess, they are doing so not without a
little . . . animation. But what do you expect? They are
no less men for being judges; and these abominable insults being showered on them by a certain section of
the press are beginning to upset them. Just imagine it,
sir; when they go home soon, they will find waiting for
them a whole pile of anonymous letters and newspapers
full of insults. . . . What a case it is! What a case! And
life used to be so quiet here!"

After twenty minutes of this chatter, an usher came
and told us that the court was resuming.

"If you are not too tired," the president said, "we
are going to interrogate you again."

So I was put back on the rack. The points to which

I was brought back most often and with the most minute curiosity were Panizzardi's telegram of November 2, 1894, my conversations with Lieutenant-Colonel Henry, and the Kaiser's alleged letters.

Before adjourning for the day, the president said to me that the Criminal Chamber would appreciate being given access to the diplomatic file, to which it attached the greatest importance. I replied:

"M. Delcassé has authorized me to inform you in advance that he will give his consent."

After a long session in the office of the clerk of the court, helping him draft the record of my evidence, I left the Palais de Justice at six o'clock, giving the slip to a pack of journalists.

I went straight to the Foreign Ministry, where I gave M. Delcassé an account of the day's proceedings.

Tuesday, January 10, 1899

These are the impressions I have taken away after my first contact with the judges of the Criminal Chamber.

In the first place, is it necessary for me to say that I found these "hirelings of Germany," these "valets of the synagogue," these "rogues in ermine," very decent people, irreproachable from the point of view of national sentiment? Even in the most heated argument, not one of them let slip the slightest word of venomous criticism of the army, or the slightest sign of ill will toward it.

At the same time, they seemed to me to bring to their

task the most scrupulous conscientiousness and the greatest keenness and courage, together with a very high sense of the formidable responsibility that is imposed on them.

The only thing in which I found them inferior to their task was their inexperience of practical life, their complete ignorance of the world, the narrowness of their horizons. The details and subleties of legal thought are, of course, not well adapted to enlarging the mind. I noticed this, for instance, when I was questioned about the Kaiser's alleged letters. Twenty minutes of explanation were required of me to make it clear to them that a royal and imperial majesty does not personally intervene in matters of espionage.

Tuesday, January 17, 1899

The Council of Ministers having decided that the diplomatic file on the Dreyfus case shall be communicated to the Cour de Cassation, Delcassé has given me the following instructions:

(1) M. Paléologue will personally exhibit each document, commenting upon it in accordance with the questions put to him.

(2) He will not permit the taking of any copy or extract of any document; but to facilitate the further deliberations of the judges, he will not object to their taking note of the serial number which will be written on each document.

The submission of the file will no doubt take several days, because it includes no fewer than two hundred documents.

Wednesday, January 18, 1899

For some days the battle between Dreyfusards and Nationalists has been raging again. Abuse, slander, anathemas, threats, challenges, have been flying backward and forward between the two camps with hideous violence.

The fever of public passions has invaded the precincts of the law: it has even penetrated the closed doors of the court where the Criminal Chamber is sitting. Each day's sitting is marked by some more or less scandalous incident. Military witnesses are to be seen emerging from the court with purple faces and abuse on their lips, alleging they have been bullied or roughly handled by the judges, who in turn accuse the officers of arrogance and defiance.

Things have got to such a pitch that a Nationalist deputy has tabled in Parliament a resolution which would withdraw from the Criminal Chamber the right of pronouncing judgment on the case and transfer it to the three Chambers sitting jointly.

Such interference with a case in progress would be no less than a breach of legal principles, and I can imagine in what terms it would be stigmatized by an English Lord Chief Justice or Attorney-General. But in the exceptional, I might almost say revolutionary, circumstances through which our country is passing, is there any other way of obtaining a decision that will be universally accepted?

Thursday, January 19, 1899

A fine thought of St. Augustine's, which it does one good to read in these days, is the following: "How can it be?" says the Bishop of Hippo in his *Confessions,* "how can it be that truth engenders hatred? .... It is because it is so well loved that those very men who love something that is opposed to it claim that that something is the truth. And, as they hate being wrong, they hate him who wishes to convince them of their error. Thus what they believe to be the truth makes them hate the truth itself."

Friday, January 20, 1899

My second appearance before the Criminal Chamber.

First of all I handed to M. Loew, the president, two documents that the Italian Ambassador, "desirous of contributing to the establishment of the truth," has just sent officially to Delcassé.

The first of these documents is a copy of a message sent by Panizzardi on November 1, 1894, to General Marselli, the Italian Chief of Staff, informing him of Dreyfus' arrest. The message said: "I hasten to assure you that this individual has never had anything to do with me. My German colleague knows no more about him than I. I do not know if Dreyfus had dealings with the General Staff."

The second document is General Marselli's telegraphed reply: "The General Staff and the services subordinate to it have never had any dealings direct or indirect with Captain Dreyfus."

My submission to the court of these documents led to a long buzz of whispering among the judges. I then began going through the diplomatic file, which contained confirmation of everything I had said in my evidence.

Wednesday, January 25, 1899

My third appearance before the Criminal Chamber. The scrutiny of the diplomatic file continued.

There was a very close, sometimes even rather sharp, discussion of the telegram of November 2, 1894, provoked by the evidence recently given by General Gonse who, in spite of all that I had said to him and all that he had honestly confessed to me, had not hesitated to state under oath that the genuine version of this telegram was damning to Dreyfus.

And that inclines me more and more to believe that a bogus version of the telegram was among the documents surreptitiously communicated to the members of the 1894 court-martial.

Friday, January 27, 1899

My evidence in the Criminal Chamber is to be submitted to the Minister of War to give the officers mentioned an opportunity to reply. This is not a regular procedure from the point of view of legal doctrine, but from my own personal point of view I could see no objection. Perhaps I was wrong.

For several days past the militarist press has been spreading a strange rumor. According to this, the statements made by me in court should be accepted only with the greatest reserve, not because I was speaking what I did not believe to be the truth, but because I did not know what really happened in 1894; I knew only the surface, the facade, the outward mask; like so many others, I was the dupe of official lies. Only one person knew everything, all the secrets of the terrible affair, *e.g.,* the agonizing events of the "tragic night" and the true version of the Panizzardi telegram and the Kaiser's letters. That person was my young colleague Delaroche-Vernet, now an embassy secretary in Berlin.

He must be very astonished at the role attributed to him.

He helped in deciphering the Panizzardi telegram in 1894, but I am not aware that he was otherwise concerned with the Dreyfus trial and the subsequent events. I admit, however, that by his mysterious manner and the rather affected reserve of his behavior he may unconsciously have provided some pretext for the absurd legend that has just grown up.

However that may be, Delcassé, wishing to anticipate any possible surprises, has decided to send me to Berlin to question Delaroche-Vernet.

I am leaving tomorrow; our Ambassador, the Mar-

quis de Noailles, is offering me hospitality, the better
to preserve the secret of my journey.[3]

Berlin, Sunday, January 29, 1899

I officially interrogated Delaroche-Vernet.

In regard to the telegram of November 2, 1894, he
confirmed my evidence in the Criminal Chamber in detail and in the most categorical terms.

I then asked him:

"Have you ever had knowledge of a letter said to
have been addressed by the Kaiser to Count Münster
relating to the Dreyfus case?"

"No, never."

"Have you ever had knowledge of a letter addressed
by the Kaiser to Captain Dreyfus?"

"No, never."

"Have you at any time addressed any written communication about the Dreyfus case to officers of the
Ministry of War?"

"No, never."

We drew up a signed statement to the above effect.

When I showed it to the old Marquis de Noailles,
who is the embodiment of shrewdness and intelligence,
he shrugged his shoulders.

"Tell me, are they mad in Paris?" he exclaimed.
"How can any newspaper be so idiotic as to suggest
that the Emperor of Germany wrote to a spy in his

[3] Emmanuel, Marquis de Noailles (1830–1909) was in turn French
Minister in Washington (1872), Minister and then Ambassador to
the Quirinal in Rome (1873–82), Ambassador in Constantinople
(1882–86), and finally Ambassador in Berlin (1896–1902).

THE COUR DE CASSATION

own hand? And what is even more remarkable, how can
anyone be so idiotic as to believe such rubbish? It's
more ridiculous than the most preposterous serial
novel!''

I dined and spent the whole evening alone with him.
He questioned me at length about the political views of
Delcassé, of whose adroitness he has a high opinion,
but he fears he may commit himself too deeply to Russia.

"The Russian alliance," he said, "should be kept
within the wise limits set for it by its sponsors. Between ourselves, I believe it is deviating a little too
much from its original aim. It was conceived as an in-
strument of peace, equilibrium, and security; but it
also contains war in its flanks. Don't forget that. And
since M. Delcassé likes working with you, remind him
of it from time to time!''

In conclusion, he explained to me his ideas about
the advantages of Franco-German co-operation. He
considered that the problems in Africa, the inevitable
dismemberment of the Portuguese colonies, the immi-
nent conflict between Britain and the Transvaal, provided a natural opportunity for a *rapprochement* between France and Germany.

"And what would you do about Alsace-Lorraine in
such a *rapprochement?*" I asked the Ambassador. "I
take the liberty of asking you that question because
it is the first question that M. Delcassé would put to
you.''

He raised his arms in a frightened manner.

"Oh!...Oh!'' he exclaimed. "About that I've nothing

to say. It's outside my sphere. Alsace-Lorraine is not a diplomatic question!''

We ventured no farther on that dangerous territory.

I leave Berlin at 1 P.M. tomorrow and return direct to Paris.

Tuesday, January 31, 1899

I made my fourth appearance before the Criminal Chamber.

In the waiting-room, which is situated in one of the medieval towers, I found Hanotaux and General Mercier. They were walking up and down without speaking to each other. At the end of the room, standing at the corner of a cupboard and looking as if he were doing penance, was poor General Gonse.

I went from one to the other, and then sat down next to Hanotaux, who muttered a number of broken, insignificant phrases, his fingers twitching nervously.

My admiration for General Mercier's haughty and unperturbed self-control was all the greater. Nothing had been able to shake his faith in his own infallibility. The ruins that had accumulated round his handiwork, the most categorical denials, the most devastating disclosures, the troubled consciences of many of the most upright and able men, left him unmoved. *Impavidum ferient ruinae....* Moreover, there is something satanic about his angular, haughty, icy face. He is a Dantesque character; he reminds me of that magnificent example of human pride, Farinata degli Uberti, who in the infernal circle drew himself up to his full height and looked about him in supreme disdain, "as if he held hell in great contempt," *Come avesse lo Inferno in gran dispitto.* But now the Criminal Chamber claimed me.

Wednesday, February 1, 1899

Now I have no more doubt that a faked version of the Panizzardi telegram was among the documents surreptitiously communicated to the members of the 1894 court.

But, as it is only a personal deduction, have I the right to give evidence to that effect?

Thursday, February 2, 1899

Esterhazy, who has taken refuge in Holland, has appeared before the Criminal Chamber during the past few days. Having had a nasty collision with French justice because of a slight case of swindling, the bully was able to come and give evidence only under the protection of a safe-conduct.

According to what I was told at the clerk's office, to which I was summoned this morning, the judges were dumfounded and overwhelmed by his boastings and braggings, the fantastic nonsense he talked, his cynical and ferocious irrepressibility.

As for the real substance of the case, he skillfully evaded awkward questions. He maintained that he had been "the General Staff's man" in his dealings with Schwartzkoppen but did not admit authorship of the *bordereau.* Then he declared, "with due deference to

200

the highest court in France," that he would unbosom himself another day, when the time had come. Finally, he delivered an endless tirade against his former chiefs, patrons, or sponsors whom he described as dunces, ignoramuses, and cowards, and a pack of ungrateful humbugs.

The consequence is that Nationalist circles affect to ignore his evidence.

Friday, February 3, 1899

My fifth appearance before the Criminal Chamber.

I arrived there at two o'clock, and had to wait a few minutes in the clerk's office. Suddenly the door burst open.

It was General Roget who had just completed his evidence. His face was scarlet, his eyes were bursting out of his head, his fists were clenched, and he was foaming with rage.

"The rogues! The scoundrels!" he exclaimed. "Doubting the word of a French officer! Setting the word of a German officer against it! Corrupt lot of traitors! This has got to stop, by . . . !"

While the clerk, who was trembling with fear, led me rapidly toward the courtroom, I recalled a striking unfinished phrase from Pascal which, in its picturesque conciseness, sums up the whole atmosphere of the *Fronde:* "When force attacks pretension, when a simple soldier takes the square cap of a presiding judge and flings it out of the window! . . ."

When I entered the court the judges were still in a

state of agitation; they were talking in low voices, and there was indignation in the glances that they exchanged. The court was full of something like an atmosphere of battle.

Friday, February 10, 1899

The rabid campaign that the Nationalist newspapers have been conducting for more than two months against the Criminal Chamber has borne fruit.

Charles Dupuy, the Prime Minister, whose courage is not his primary virtue, has just had a bill passed at the Palais Bourbon removing the case from the jurisdiction of the Criminal Chamber and transferring it to the three Chambers sitting together.

This departure from all rules of procedure, this arbitrary incursion by the political power into the realm of justice, is too shocking for it to be possible to derive the slightest satisfaction from it.

Public passions are going to be still more roused. The abominable dispute is going on; on the one hand, contempt of liberal ideas, appeals to force, offenses against justice; on the other, a progressive darkening of the national conscience and the French mentality. You have to go back to the saddest hours of our history to find a parallel to this tragic discord.

Friday, February 17, 1899

Yesterday evening, at about six o'clock, President Félix Faure had an apoplectic fit, of which he died at ten o'clock. The cause of death, according to the certificate signed by the doctors who were hastily summoned, was "lightning cerebral hemorrhage with paralysis of the face and the limbs of the left side."

Between four and five o'clock he had received Cardinal Richard, the Archbishop of Paris, and Prince Albert of Monaco; then he had signed some decrees.

His death has caused consternation among the Nationalists, whose enterprises he surreptitiously aided and abetted; the "law of disseizin" can be said to owe much to his personal influence. From the point of view of foreign politics, his disappearance is not a negligible event; he filled his ornamental role with dignity, and though he played the sovereign a little too much, his judgment in diplomatic matters was farsighted and shrewd.

Saturday, February 18, 1899

The President of the Senate, Émile Loubet, has been elected President of the Republic.

His election, which was never in doubt, is considered by the Nationalists an "insult to France," a "challenge to the army," and a "victory for Jewish treason."

The new President, "the elect of the synagogue," arrived at the Gare St. Lazare at about five o'clock and went to the Élysée to pay his respects beside the coffin of his predecessor; he then came to the Ministry of Foreign Affairs, where the ceremonial investiture with the Presidential powers took place.

He was pursued all along the route by the whistles,

hisses, and boos of the patriotic and anti-Semitic leagues.

When the procession at last reached the steps of the Quai d'Orsay, the din was such that my colleagues and I were unable to hear a single note of the Marseillaise, which was played by a military band within twenty paces of us.[4]

Tuesday, February 21, 1899

In the present over-heated state of public passions, the death of Félix Faure led inevitably to the wildest suspicions, the most fantastic rumors. Besides, the first close glance at the official announcement was sufficient to reveal that it was full of improbabilities and contradictions.

The Nationalist newspapers hinted the next day that the "great friend of the army, the courageous opponent of the reopening of the Dreyfus case," had perished at the hands of the Jews—whether by poison, revolver, or dagger was not yet known. But soon they became more positive; the death had not occurred at the Élysée, but at a mysterious house where the "dear President" had been lured by some "Judith or Delilah." Then suddenly, as if at a word of command, complete silence fell.

It was, indeed, better for our "dear President's" memory that too much light should not be shed on the circumstances of his death.

[4] The Nationalists blamed Émile Loubet for having tried to hush up the Panama scandal when he was Prime Minister in 1892. He was received in Paris with shouts of "Panama!"

I have just learned the details from Casimir-Perier, who had them from his old butler Joseph, who has remained in contact with the servants at the Élysée.

On February 16 then, at five o'clock in the evening, after receiving the Prince of Monaco and signing some decrees, Félix Faure was left alone in his office, which is on the ground floor in the left wing of the palace, backing on to the garden. To reach it you have to pass through a corner room, which is permanently occupied by Le Gall, the chief of the civil secretariat. Beyond the President's office is an elegant boudoir, the last room in the Presidential suite.

At about half-past five a young woman arrived, Mme Steinheil, whose husband has some reputation as a portrait painter.

Mme Steinheil, who is very pretty, fascinating and wanton, and very expert in what Guy de Maupassant called the "art of breaking men's backs," had for some time held the President infatuated by the heady philter of her skillful ardors. Now, the handsome Félix, in spite of his slender figure and sturdy chest, was not less than fifty-nine years old, and more than once people had had occasion to notice his glassy eyes, his puffy eyelids, and his sudden stumbling over words. It is even said that not long since he had had some ill-boding congestive trouble. He had thus passed the age for making Mme Steinheil's acquaintance; for she was one of those women whose acquaintance one does not make with impunity.

However that may be, at about a quarter to seven Le Gall, in the course of his docile and pathetic guard-

ing of the door to the Presidential office, thought he
heard strange, stifled cries coming from the boudoir.

He went nearer; then, no longer doubting that something serious had happened, he decided to force the
locked door.

And what did he find? The President unconscious,
in a fit, in the most significant state of undress, and
near him, entirely naked, Mme Steinheil, screaming,
hysterical, and frantic.

Before rushing for help, he desired to re-establish
a little order. But, apart from the fact that Mme Steinheil was twisting and writhing in an uncontrollable
manner, the President was clutching her hair in his
clenched fist.

After long and vain efforts, Le Gall rang for an
usher, who hurried to fetch a servant.

Mme Steinheil gradually calmed down and dressed
herself again; she was hurried away down the unob-
trusive passageway that runs along the little interior
court. Then, as best they could, they laid the still unconscious President on a sofa.

Finally, when decency had been restored, Mme Faure
was informed, and doctors were sent for. By this time
it was half-past seven.

Dr. Lannelongue and Dr. Potain arrived immediately; they diagnosed cerebral hemorrhage and did not
disguise the fact that the end was near.

A guard was sent hurriedly to fetch the priest from
La Madeleine. But a priest, a prison chaplain, happened to be passing the Élysée, and the guard stopped
him and took him into the palace and to the dying man;

the priest pronounced the words of absolution used in extreme urgency when the dying man is no longer able to confess: *"Absolvo te, in quantum ego possum et tu indiges, in nomine Patris filii et Spiritus Sancti. Amen."* "In so far as I am able and thou hast need, I absolve thee in the name of the Father, the Son, and the Holy Ghost. Amen." At ten o'clock Félix Faure died.

Monday, February 27, 1899

A lively, almost personal, argument has been going on for some days between the Minister of War and his colleague, the Minister of Foreign Affairs. Once more it is concerned with the famous telegram of November 2, 1894, because the General Staff is desperately trying to maintain the genuineness of the version faked by Henry which is the foundation on which rests the whole scaffolding of sophisms, inferences, and lies that caused Dreyfus to be convicted.

Captain Cuignet, at a loss for a reply to the conclusive evidence in the matter that I gave to the Criminal Chamber, did not hesitate officially to impugn the good faith of the Minister of Foreign Affairs.

Delcassé took up the matter as soon as he was informed of it by the Keeper of the Seals, and an exchange of letters with Freycinet followed. Three times the incident seemed to have been closed, but each time the impetuous and virulent Cuignet roused the whole pack of patriotic newspapers against his Minister, and each time this statesman—so intelligent, so able, and so weak—agreed to reopen the exhausted controversy. Things have got to such a pitch that Delcassé has just sent his pusillanimous colleague a very stiff letter indeed in which he says that he will not allow his department to be slandered by an officer holding an official position, and that consequently he is having all the documents submitted to the three Chambers of the Cour de Cassation sitting in joint session. "The question will be clearly put," he wrote. "Were the subsequent amendments to the first version of the telegram of November 2, 1894, justified or not? The question must be clearly answered. Did Colonel Sandherr verify the correctness of the amended text, yes or no? . . . . The Supreme Court, thus instructed, will decide if good faith was on the side of my department or on that of M. Cuignet."

I was proposing to go to Italy for a fortnight and was counting on leaving tomorrow. In view of the circumstances, I told Delcassé that I was prepared to postpone my departure. He replied cordially:

"No, no! Leave tomorrow. I am only too delighted at your having a little rest; you have well deserved it."

From Tuesday, February 28, to Thursday, March 16, 1899

Trip to Florence, Rome, and Nervi . . . .
. . . .

As at this time last year, I note that the Dreyfus case has deeply moved the Italian imagination. The slightest incidents and developments are seized on and discussed with an interest that does not flag. But what the Italians find most astonishing is that Henry's suicide did not open everybody's eyes in France, and they do not understand how it is possible that the majority, the vast majority, of the French people should still believe Dreyfus to be guilty. Moreover Barrère, our Ambassador to the Italian court, told me that in Government and military circles alike no hesitation is felt in admitting that Esterhazy was in Schwartzkoppen's and Panizzardi's pay; some initiates even add *sotto voce* that Henry was an accomplice in the treasonable activity.

At the Vatican and in "black" circles Dreyfus' guilt is no longer regarded as an axiomatic and self-evident truth. It is no longer claimed that the Jews were created by a special decree of Providence so that noble causes should never lack their traitors. Words are now weighed, and the attitude is guarded. In this respect, that magnanimous and liberal Christian, Leo XIII is setting a courageous example. When he gave an audience recently to Boyer d'Agen, a French religious writer, he said to him: "Why is chivalrous France using up the best of her strength in this frightful struggle, which is without glory for her and without profit for suffering humanity? Why does she not ponder the sublime lesson of Calvary a little more?"

Wednesday, March 29, 1899

At midday I appeared before the Cour de Cassation, sitting in joint session of all its Chambers, in the *grand-chambre,* which opens on to the Place Dauphine, the principal door of which opens to Harlay's lobby.

The hall, of modern construction, is sumptuously decorated in the glittering Roman *palazzo* style; there are too many accessories, too many mouldings, too much foliage, too many garlands, too many allegorical scenes. Among all this richness all the charm of the clear harmonies of Paul Baudry's glorious ceiling, "The Apotheosis of the Law," is lost.

Fifty judges were present, including the public prosecutor; their seats occupied three sides of the hall.

I took my seat to the left of the presiding judge Mazeau; on my left was Tanon, presiding judge of the Chamber of Pleas. Next to him was Manau, the Procurator-General, and next Desjardins, the Advocate-General. To the right of the presiding judge, I noticed Loew, the presiding judge of the Criminal Chamber, and finally, Ballot-Beaupré, the president of the Civil Chamber, who has been appointed judge-advocate for the case at issue.

While the clerk of the court read a brief procedural document in a nasal voice, I thought of the tremendous picture painted for us by Macaulay of the House of Lords assembled for the trial of Warren Hastings: "The place was worthy of such a trial. It was the great hall of William Rufus, etc., etc."

But by a sudden quirk of memory, I simultaneously recalled that the old pamphleteer Rochefort, who for thirty years has not tired of stirring up hatred and spreading calumny, recently dared to write: "I should like to have all the judges of the Supreme Court drawn up behind one another like a string of sausages, like convicts in jail. Then a well-trained hangman would cut off their eyelids and slowly empty the sockets of their eyes. Afterward they would be exposed on a big pillory in the Place Dauphine, with this inscription: 'This is how France punishes traitors who betray her to Germany.'"

When the clerk had finished his nasal reading, the presiding judge invited me "to produce and disclose all that is known to the Ministry of Foreign Affairs about the Dreyfus case."

I started with the documents and information that established the role of Germany in the crime of 1894.

The discussion was very close, very meticulous, and at times even very heated, and lasted for no less than an hour and three-quarters.

I next came to the documents and information that threw light on the role of Italy. When I came to the telegram of November 2, 1894, there was a kind of redoubling of attention all round me. Most of the judges took notes. After each sentence, I was asked questions, pressed to explain what I was saying, to produce my evidence, to justify my statements. I thus led the court to recognition of the absolute accuracy of the only translation of that telegram that the Foreign Ministry had ever put forward as genuine. Its accuracy had been confirmed by a supplementary check put in hand by Colonel Sandherr, and the text was as follows: "If Captain Dreyfus has not had dealings with you, it would be advisable to instruct the Ambassador to publish an official denial to avoid comments in the press.''

Finally I demonstrated by what stratagems and devices this so definite text had been transformed in the War Ministry file into document No. 44 reading: ''Captain Dreyfus has been arrested. The War Minister has proof of his relations with Germany. I have taken all precautions.''

I concluded in these terms:

''Thus my conscience and my instructions oblige me to say that document No. 44 is not just an incorrect translation; it is a falsification.''

Tumult in court! For about ten minutes, I was assailed by objections and questions which I had no difficulty in answering.

At four o'clock the court adjourned. The presiding judge, after thanking me for my ''so important, so grave'' evidence, said to me:

''I am afraid we shall have to ask you to appear before us again very soon.''

Thursday, March 30, 1899

My appearance in court yesterday, the four hours during which I was under the cross-fire of fifty judges, while I had continually to draw on my memory, improvise my replies, weigh all my words, have left me with a great exhaustion of spirit.

The official record of evidence, which I have just signed at the Palais de Justice, no more reproduces the feel of the proceedings than a post-mortem report gives a picture of life.

For the long deliberation was very agitated.

If I must pay homage to the calm and scrupulous impartiality of the presiding judge, I cannot speak so highly of the others.

It was only too plain that the court was divided into two camps. Several times discussion degenerated into argument, and remarks, objections, replies were exchanged in such a harsh and angry tone that I might have been at a political meeting and not in a court of justice.

What shocked me much more were the remarks that certain judges whispered into my ear during the two brief adjournments. One said to me: "Bravo, sir! Go on! Go to the root of the matter!" Another said: "How grateful we are to you, sir! You bring us a great light. It is like tearing a veil from our eyes!" A third, on the contrary, said: "Oh, sir, weigh your words well! Don't let yourself go too far! There are persons here whose outlook is so unwholesome!"

And finally Tanon, the president of the Chamber of Pleas, who was seated on my left, goaded me continually. With his hand over his mouth, he kept muttering such things as: "What you have just said is vital. Go on! Go on!" "See how moved the court is. Hold firm!" "Don't leave it at that! Draw the consequences!" "If you have scruples about disclosing your personal conclusions, at least indicate them to us in the form of hypotheses!" I pretended not to hear any of these invitations.

To end on a commendatory note, however, let me say that several judges struck me by their demeanor, their reserve, their gravity. Thus the presiding judges Loew and Ballot-Beaupré, and the judges Voisin, Dareste, Roullier, Attahalin seemed to me to be in the fine tradition of Harlay, Pasquier, and Lamoignon.

Saturday, April 8, 1899

When I returned home this evening, I found this letter waiting for me, bearing the stamp of the Ministry of Foreign Affairs:

SIR,

I have taken cognizance of the evidence you have been called on to give in the Dreyfus case as the representative of the Ministry of Foreign Affairs, both before the Criminal Chamber and before all the Chambers of the Cour de Cassation sitting in joint session.

I have noted that in the evidence you have given you did not at any time depart from my instructions, and I have appreciated the reserve, the tact, and the moderation that you succeeded in observing in dealing with the particularly delicate matters that you had to elucidate before the Cour de Cassation.

In these circumstances I have pleasure in expressing to you in an altogether special manner my complete satisfaction with the manner in which you carried out the task that was entrusted to you.

Yours, etc.
(signed) DELCASSÉ

Tuesday, April 18, 1899

For the past fortnight the Nationalist press has naturally been covering me with insults, of which the kindest are: "Traitor and liar," "forger," "virtuoso of imposture, dilettante of crime," and "German agent." It is not offensive; it is not even irritating; it is sad and ugly. If I had need of consolation, I should have only to think of the words of La Bruyère: "Those who think badly of us without knowing enough about us do us no wrong; it is not us that they attack, but a phantom of their own imagination."

Thursday, April 20, 1899

The terrible Cuignet, who has just been promoted major and has become the standard-bearer of the General Staff, has bullied poor Freycinet so unmercifully that he has succeeded in causing him to have another clash with Delcassé, and thus there has been another exchange of acrimonious letters between the two Ministers.

The Cour de Cassation, apprised of the matter, has summoned me tomorrow morning for a confrontation with General Chamoin, who will speak in the name of the Minister of War.

Friday, April 21, 1899

At midday I appeared before the joint session of the three Chambers with General Chamoin, the representative of the War Ministry.

After a long, lively, and very courteous argument,

in which I maintained all my positions, the court ordered that the telegram of November 2, 1894, should be deciphered afresh by me in the presence of General Chamoin, Major Cuignet, and Ménard, the clerk of the court.

Thursday, April 27, 1899

General Chamoin, Major Cuignet, and I met today in the chambers of the presiding judge of the Cour de Cassation to have the Panizzardi telegram deciphered all over again in the presence of Ménard, the clerk of the court.

Without the slightest difficulty, and without provoking the slightest contradiction, I caused the following to emerge from the cryptogram: "If Captain Dreyfus has not had dealings with you, it would be advisable to instruct the Ambassador to publish an official denial to avoid comments in the press."

At the conclusion of this operation, the clerk drew up a report, to which the representatives of the War Office and I added our signatures. General Chamoin complied with a good grace; Major Cuignet was quivering with rage.

Monday, May 1, 1899

Dinner at the house of Grégoire Ghika, the Rumanian Minister.

At dinner my neighbors were Mme Ghika, whose sister is the Queen of Serbia, and the exquisite Mme de Weede, wife of the Counselor of the Netherlands Legation.

This charming Dutchwoman, with her feline movements and big, passionate eyes, naturally does not know that I have read all her love letters to Schwartzkoppen—a file of eighty letters of which the recipient was relieved by a skillful spy employed by the intelligence service. She started talking to me about the Dreyfus case over the soup. I evaded her questions as much as possible, saying that the case was full of obscurities and that I still had doubts about Dreyfus' innocence. "What!" she exclaimed. "You talk like that! You!" Her eyes flashed with astonishment and indignation. Her voice gradually rose, and she spoke with such ardor that everybody stopped talking to listen to her. Suddenly she stopped and grew thoughtful, as if a thought had suddenly struck her. "It's strange!" she went on. "My husband no longer believes in Dreyfus' innocence either!" I should have liked to point out to her that neither her husband nor I had had at our disposal such powerful means as she had had to extract from Schwartzkoppen the truth about the Dreyfus case. Remembering some of the intimate letters she had written to him, I could well imagine what spells and enchantments she had used to extract all the handsome Prussian officer's secrets.

> *Facie tenerisque lacertis*
> *Devovet . . . .*

Monday, May 29, 1899

I met Paul Bourget in the Rue François I, at about two o'clock this afternoon. It was nearly six months since I had last seen him.

He greeted me with affectionate anger.

"I disown you as a friend," he said. "I wish to have no more to do with you. You disgraced yourself in accepting that task; you should have resigned. You have put your personal honesty in the service of a gang of bandits. That Delcassé is the worst of scoundrels. . . . Oh, yes! I know what you are going to say—the cause of justice. Well, I don't care a fig for justice! Remember Goethe's admirable saying at the siege of Mainz: 'I prefer an injustice to a disorder?' "

I interrupted him.

"You have put the answer into my mouth," I said. "In a well-ordered society there is only one thing for an official duly summoned before a court of law to do: to testify according to his conscience. That is what I have done."

After this we walked together as far as the Rue Constantine, talking about literature. Paul Bourget left me outside the entrance to the Foreign Ministry with the words:

"I like you all the same!"

Saturday, June 3, 1899

Today the joint session of the three Chambers of the Cour de Cassation, the judges sitting in red robes, unanimously pronounced judgment quashing Dreyfus' conviction of December 22, 1894, and sending him back for retrial by court-martial at Rennes.

5. RENNES
COURT-MARTIAL

5 . RENNES
COURT-MARTIAL

Tuesday, August 1, 1899

The Government,[1] having decided that I should submit the diplomatic file on the Dreyfus case to the Rennes court-martial, the Foreign Minister relieved me of the duty of official secrecy, leaving me to be my own judge of the restrictions required of me by state security.

The case is to open on August 7 and is expected to take about twenty days.[2]

Delcassé is leaving tomorrow for St. Petersburg to

[1] This was Waldeck-Rousseau's Government, formed on June 22, 1899, which remained in office until June 4, 1902. General de Galliffet was War Minister until May 28, 1900, when he was succeeded by General André.

[2] It in fact took twenty-nine days, from August 7 to September 9.

return the visit to Paris paid by Count Muraviev last autumn.

These last days I have been working directly under his orders, preparing for his St. Petersburg conversations. His chief aim is to introduce into the Franco-Russian pact a clause by which the military convention of 1892 would no longer be tied to the existence of the opposing coalition but would remain in force "even in the event of a dissolution of the Triple Alliance." Delcassé, in fact, secretly cherishes the dream of luring Italy away from the Teutonic powers. I have drawn up two memoranda on this subject for him to use in his conversations with the Czar and Muraviev. . . .

Sunday, August 6, 1899

I arrived at Rennes at four o'clock, with General Chamoin. Two Sûreté detectives accompanied us from Paris to guard the bags that contain the secret documents.

From the station we went straight to the court-martial office, where we deposited our documents. Two rooms have been put at our disposal, with barred windows opening on to a yard of the military prison. The door is guarded night and day by a sentry with fixed bayonet.

From there we drove to the Hôtel Moderne, on the Quai Lamennais, on the banks of the Vilaine, whose waters flow as black as ink, *Stygios fluctus*. . . . The cleanliness of the rooms reserved for us by the prefect is impeccable.

After a wash, we went together to pay our official respects to the army corps commander, General Lucas; to the prefect of Ile-et-Vilaine, Duréault; to the presiding officer at the court-martial, Colonel Jouaust; and to the prosecuting officer, Major Carrière. Finally we had a look at the secondary school hall in which the court will sit.

The usual court-martial room is indeed far too small for the big trial that is about to take place. One of the big rooms of the Palais de Justice might have been chosen—for instance the old *grand-chambre* so magnificently decorated by Coypel, in which the parliament of Brittany used to sit. But preference was given to the school hall because of its proximity to the military prison, which will make it much easier to take Dreyfus backward and forward daily.

The building, which is huge and of modern construction, stands on the very spot where the famous Jesuit college, the most important in the kingdom, once stood; and as soon as I entered I was haunted by the thought of Chateaubriand; it was here that in his fifteenth year he experienced his first troubles: "I heard the distant and seductive voices of the passions coming to me; I threw myself in the way of these sirens, attracted by an unknown harmony. . . ." But I had other things to do than summon up the ghost of René. In the hall where the court-martial is to sit, I found the director of the Sûreté Générale, a colonel of the General Staff, five police superintendents, twelve officers of *gendarmerie,* and about sixty *gendarmes* and policemen busily applying finishing touches in readiness for tomorrow.

224

The arrangements leave nothing to be desired. Chamoin and I are to sit on the platform behind the
judges.

"Hasn't everything been well arranged?" the prefect Duréault, who had just arrived, said to me in a
friendly manner.

"Yes, the scenery is perfect," I replied. "All we are
waiting for now is the rising of the curtain."

But privately I wondered whether such an enormous,
such a resounding, such a theatrical hall did not involve the risk of transforming the proceedings into a
play and exaggerating still further the dramatic elements in the case, which ought to be decided in cool and
calm surroundings.

The prefect, as if to reinforce me in that opinion,
started telling me how anxious he was about the state
of feeling at Rennes, into which the champions and
fanatics of the two rival camps were pouring.

"You cannot imagine the violence of the altercations
that have already taken place in the cafés and the
streets," he said. "What will it be like after the case
has begun? You'll see that it'll end in blows!"

Chamoin and I, being determined to preserve the
neutrality imposed on us by our official position, have
decided to keep severely apart from the belligerents.
We shall avoid public places and take all our meals together in a private room at the Hôtel Moderne. Only
Captain Moreau, the general's aide-de-camp, and my
secretary, the Vicomte du Halgouët, an embassy attaché, will share our table.[3]

[3] The court-martial was constituted as follows: Presiding officer:

Monday, August 7, 1899

At 6:50 A.M. General Chamoin and I entered the court room. Two chairs were reserved for us behind those to be occupied by the judges.

The prosecuting officer, Major Carrière, who arrived at the same time we did, took his seat to the left of the court. Opposite us the counsel for Dreyfus, Maître Demange and Maître Labori, in caps and black robes, spread their piles of papers on a long table. In front of them were two empty chairs—one for the prisoner, and the other for the captain of *gendarmes,* his escort.

The huge hall was crammed; at least a thousand people were present. All had the same pale faces, drawn with excitement; no one but was fascinated by the small, low door, to the left of the platform, where two *gendarmes* were on guard, for everyone guessed that it was from there that Dreyfus would emerge.

In front of me, at the foot of the platform, were the crowd of witnesses, about a hundred officers and about twenty civilians. Crowding the rest of the hall in front of me, even sitting on the window sills, were the public, the press, many soldiers, many foreigners, many priests, many women.

Among the serried ranks of witnesses, I saw a former

Colonel Jouaust, director of engineering to the 10th Army Corps. Members of the court: Lieutenant-Colonel Brongniart, director of artillery, 10th Army Corps; Majors de Bréon and Merle, of the 7th Regiment of Artillery; Major Profillet, of the 10th Regiment of Artillery; Captains Parfait and Beauvais, of the 7th Regiment of Artillery.

President of the Republic, five former Ministers of War, four former civilian Ministers, a former Chief of the General Staff, and innumerable generals, colonels, majors, and captains.

How many ruins and wrecks there were among them! All those whom the Dreyfus case has morally killed were there; it was like a necropolis. Two witnesses were missing, however: Esterhazy, who has taken refuge in London; and Henry, who has taken refuge in death.

Seven o'clock struck. There was a brief word of command. Everyone rose, and the guard presented arms.

The seven members of the court, in full dress uniform, filed in. When they reached the platform, they returned the guard's salute and took their seats.

The presiding officer, Colonel Jouaust, who has a hard, martial, and intelligent face, declared the court open. Then, in a dry voice, he ordered the prisoner to be brought in.

In a silence in which the whole hall seemed to hold its breath, the small door opened. Dreyfus came in, walking stiffly. He mounted the platform, saluted mechanically, and took his seat, carrying his head high, his face expressionless.

There was a strange amazement in everybody's eyes, as if they found it hard to believe that this was really Dreyfus. From afar, from the mystery of his infernal island, this man, round whose head so much hatred and pity have accumulated in the past five years, seemed, indeed, a symbol, an abstraction. For some he was a traitor, Judas, the personification of disloyalty; for

others he was the personification of innocence immo-
lated in the interests of a caste, the victim of a new Calvary, of the most monstrous crime ever committed
against justice and truth.

Now here he was, in flesh and blood, wearing a uniform, with gold braid on his sleeves, booted and
spurred. . . . But how worn and emaciated he was, what
a wreck of a human being he was reduced to! His arms
were withered, his knees so thin that they seemed to
pierce the cloth of his trousers. There were just a few
white hairs on his bald pate. Only the staring eyes behind his pince-nez gave some slight animation to his
cadaverous face. *Ecce homo!*

Meanwhile Coupois, the clerk of the court, read some
procedural documents, the arraignment, the solemn
judgment of the Cour de Cassation, and finally the
charge, the same as that of 1894. Dreyfus listened, completely immobile. But suddenly, when he heard the
same charge repeated after five years, I saw some big
tears in his eyes, which overflowed on to his cheeks.
But he immediately resumed his impassive mask, his
poor, worn-out mask, lined with pain.

The examination of the accused began. Colonel Jouaust set about it not without harshness. To all the questions put to him about the matters of which he was
accused in 1894, Dreyfus replied with denials, which he
uttered in a dry, monotonous, jerky voice.

As this dialogue continued I found a strange process
gradually taking place inside me; the sympathy for
Dreyfus with which I had at first been filled gradually
faded away and disappeared; its place was taken by a

feeling of mistrust. As it happened, Colonel Jouaust was approaching the mystery of the confession that Captain Lebrun-Renaud claimed Dreyfus had made to him on January 5, 1895, a few minutes before the degradation. Dreyfus, whose hands were trembling, made a visible effort to brace himself. Then, in his hoarse voice, he exclaimed:

"I have never made any confession. . . . I have always declared my innocence; I have always defended my honor. . . . By the head of my wife and my children, I swear that I am innocent. . . . Sir! I swear to you that I am innocent!"

And he fell back into his chair, like an automaton, his mouth horribly contorted.

I recognized these pathetic phrases, having heard them on the sinister morning of the degradation; then they had given me the inner certainty that Dreyfus was lying. Why, now I *knew* that they were true, did they still sound so false to my ear? Why is this man incapable of putting any warmth into his words? Why in his most vigorous protestations can nothing of his soul emerge through his strangled throat? There is something incomprehensible and doomed about him, like the hero of an ancient tragedy. Looking at him, I kept repeating to myself Sophocles' exclamation of pity about Oedipus: "Unhappy! Unhappy! That is the only name that I can give thee!"

During the adjournments, the members of the court withdrew into a little courtyard belonging to the school which is exclusively reserved for them. They invited General Chamoin and me to accompany them. There we smoked cigarettes and made their acquaintance. Nothing whatever was said, of course, about the crux of the case; but there was much frankness and simplicity in the questions they put to me and in the opinions they expressed about its external aspects.

At 2 P.M. the representatives of the War Ministry and the Foreign Ministry had an appointment with the members of the court at the court-martial offices to agree on procedure.

I set up my office in a narrow room, with barrack-room tables covered with horse-blankets. Chamoin has the next room. A sentry is on duty outside the door.

The window looks out on to a little garden on the other side of which are the jailers' quarters. Old Major Carrière, the prosecuting officer, was walking up and down the garden, playing with his dog and a tame crow. He and his crow must get on well together, for having the same head formation, the same facial angle, the same brain structure, why should there be any difference in their mentality?

When I left at about five o'clock, Lieutenant-Colonel Brongniart, the deputy presiding officer, and his colleague, Major de Bréon, suggested a "short walk" along the Vilaine. I felt that they wanted to gain my confidence.

"Ours is a heavy task," Brongniart said to me. "We are being brought up against an order of things with which we are unfamiliar. So we count a great deal on your help."

They did not disguise the unfavorable impression made on them this morning by the prisoner.

Tuesday, August 8, 1899

The proceedings were *in camera.*

General Chamoin submitted the secret file of the intelligence service.

During the whole of this long process, Dreyfus remained wrapped in complete silence, only glancing indifferently at the documents that the members of the court and the lawyers examined with passionate interest. His attitude seemed to say: What have those piles of paper got to do with me?

And, indeed, in all those mysterious documents, the contents of which have troubled so many minds and given rise to so many fantastic legends, there are not twenty lines that really apply to him. The whole secret file of the intelligence department consists of nothing but apocryphal or adulterated documents; inaccurate translations; distorted evidence; fragments of foolish or fabricated gossip; scraps of paper arbitrarily fitted together, to which, like the sibylline leaves, any meaning whatever can be attached; and insignificant jottings into which profound and cabalistic meanings are read. I omit the packet of sixty-four charming and intimate letters written to Schwartzkoppen by Mme de Weede. General Chamoin, in agreement with me, and relying on my testimony in the matter, asked the court to agree not to see this correspondence, which had no connection with the Dreyfus case, and the court accepted this.

In the court office this afternoon, Major Carrière did me the honor of introducing me to his dog and his crow. In return I offered him a cigar, and we immediately became close friends. The worthy major told me some good court-martial stories—spicy stories which caused him much amusement. When we said good-by, he told me that Dreyfus was ill; he is suffering from insomnia, dizziness, sickness. Will he last to the end of the trial?

Wednesday, August 9, 1899

General Chamoin completed his submission of the secret file *in camera*.

Dreyfus did not for one moment depart from his impassive manner, his machine-like stiffness. Toward the end of the day's hearing, when the heart-rending appeals that he so often addressed from his island to the President of the Republic and General de Boisdeffre were read, the faces of the members of the court betrayed their emotion; the prisoner's face remained expressionless.

At six o'clock I went for a walk with Chamoin in the handsome avenues of Le Thabor, once the grounds of a Benedictine monastery, which again revived in me memories of Chateaubriand. We talked with complete freedom. The general said to me:

"My file made no impression on the court. It really contains too many documents that are doubtful, or prove nothing."

"And those that do prove something are spurious."

"You wouldn't have to push me very far for me to agree with you. . . . What a damnable job they've given me! I shall be lucky if I don't wreck my career over it.''

Then, in a shame-faced manner, he confessed to a transgression. "Out of clumsiness, sheer clumsiness,'' he had agreed to introduce into his file a highly suspicious document that General Mercier had surreptitiously handed to him, "like a conjurer palming a card on you.'' The lawyers had noticed it and protested, and a scandal was possible. "Oh! What a damnable job!''

But we met Viguié, the director of the Sûreté Génréale, coming out of the prefecture, where he had just received his Paris mail, and we walked a little way together. He told us about a curious shift of opinion that was becoming increasingly noticeable in the reactionary and Nationalist newspapers.

"It is directed against General Mercier,'' he said.

"Oh?''

"Yes. I have been watching this strange development for some weeks. General Mercier is being criticized for his protracted silence, his shilly-shallying, his delays in coming out with the truth, which are no longer understood. What they want him to do, in fact, is at last to let the cat out of the bag. He is being called on publicly to disclose the great and terrible secret of 1894 of which he is the sole depository, and to let no scruple inhibit him any longer. He is told that, if need be, he must violate all the rules and restrictions of diplomacy, even at the risk of war. In five minutes, by a single word, he could end the trial and deliver France from her agony. This time, if he does not come out with everything, it must mean that he has made a gross, a ridiculous mistake. That is what he is now being told by Déroulède, Galli, Barrès, Rochefort, Drumont, who used to exalt him to the skies!''

Viguié added confidentially:

''And I know, thanks to the sources of information available to the police, that in their private letters his friends are even more outspoken.''

General Chamoin, for his part, had received similar information.

''In the military circles of Rennes, and, I dare even add, among the members of the court itself, what is expected of General Mercier is a decisive disclosure, a bludgeon-stroke'' he said.

''That expression 'bludgeon-stroke' rather worries me,'' I remarked, ''because it is the expression used by Lieutenant-Colonel Henry in my presence when he referred to his 'patriotic' forgery and the Kaiser's mysterious letter. . . .''

Thursday, August 10, 1899

Today it was my turn; I submitted the diplomatic file to the court-martial.

We sat round a long table at which I occupied the place of honor next to the presiding officer. The prosecuting officer sat facing me, with Maître Labori on his right and Maître Demange next to him. The remaining places were occupied by the other members of the court and the clerk.

Dreyfus' impassivity was remarkable. While the

members of the court and the lawyers submitted all the documents that I exhibited to the most minute examination and dissection, not a word escaped from his lips and his expression did not change. But when we came to an Italian telegram that pointed to Esterhazy's guilt, he leaned over toward Labori and said:

"Did you notice? . . . That's curious."

Those were the only words he uttered in the course of four hours.

The discussion was, nevertheless, very animated. The decoded telegrams of Tornielli, Visconti-Venosta, and Panizzardi caused great surprise. But the chief point of argument, the point to which I was constantly brought back, was the great puzzle of 1894, Count Münster's protests, and his appeal to the President of the Republic. Questions were rained on me tirelessly about this, and some of them were put with a crafty indirectness. I divined that the minds of the members of the court were haunted by the mysterious document on the immediate restoration of which Germany was said to have insisted under the threat of war, that is to say, the Kaiser's letter, the document annotated by his august hand; and, as my files contained no reference whatever to this fantastic episode, the court concluded that I was concealing the truth from them or did not know it.

During an adjournment Major Profillet, Captain Beauvais, and Captain Parfait questioned me—very discreetly, it is true—about our deciphering system, our methods, and our information services. Suddenly Beauvais said to me:

"Oh! If only you would tell us all that you know!"

"But I do tell you all that I know!" I exclaimed. "I assure you on my honor!"

Major Profillet, with his fine features and elegant and reserved manners, courteously intervened.

"Don't insist, Beauvais," he said. "M. Paléologue's task is difficult enough as it is!"

Friday, August 11, 1899

I completed my submission of the diplomatic file this morning. My impressions were the same as yesterday's, and Dreyfus was equally silent.

At two o'clock this afternoon, while I was working in my office with my secretary, Du Halgouët, Lieutenant-Colonel Brongniart opened the door. His angular face, his grave and concentrated manner, his incisive speech, his frigid courtesy, rare gestures, severe manner—his whole appearance—were those of a man preoccupied with moral and religious questions, a man inwardly fashioned by military and Catholic discipline. He said to me:

"I should like to talk to you privately. Could not M. du Halgouët withdraw for a few moments?"

"I have no secrets from M. du Halgouët."

"It is not to the representative of the Minister of Foreign Affairs that I wish to speak; I wish to speak privately to M. Paléologue."

I signed to Du Halgouët and he withdrew. Brongniart went on:

"I have come to appeal to your conscience. I have

come to ask you to talk to me with complete frankness, as men of honor can and must talk to each other. During the sessions *in camera* yesterday and this morning, you showed us some very interesting documents, and you explained them clearly. But you did not once mention the personal conclusions you drew from them, either for or against Dreyfus. That greatly struck my colleagues and myself. I shall even permit myself to add that it gave all of us a very high opinion of you. Consequently I am certain that none of them would disown me if they knew of the appeal that I have come to make to you. So please tell me frankly what your opinion is on the question of Dreyfus' innocence or guilt.''

I told Brongniart how touched I was by what he had said and explained to him the reservations imposed on me by my official role, from which I had never departed, even before the Cour de Cassation.

''That is why I am addressing myself solely to your conscience as a private individual,'' he said with a touch of stiffness.

''Then it is solely as a private individual that I shall give you my answer,'' I replied.

He thanked me in a few simple, dignified words. I went on:

''If I confine myself to telling you that after firmly believing that Dreyfus was guilty, I now believe him to be innocent, you will not gain much profit from our conversation. It seems to me that I can be much more useful to you in drawing your attention to the points to which you should principally direct your attention as the trial proceeds: for these points, in my opinion, throw light on the whole of the Dreyfus case.''

He installed himself at the corner of my table to take notes. I went on:

''The first point to clear up is the arrival of the *bordereau*. In what circumstances was it abstracted from the German Embassy? I assure you that Schwartzkoppen never received it. Clear up the ridiculous legend of the 'Kaiser's letter'; force those who created it to explain why they did so. Ask General de Boisdeffre and General Gonse what their opinion was on the question of Dreyfus' guilt or innocence in October, 1896, when Lieutenant-Colonel Henry decided to commit his forgery for the sole purpose of deceiving them and nobody else. Get Mme Henry to tell you to what persons (I insist on the plural) her husband referred in his last letter when he wrote: 'You know in *whose* interest I acted.' Finally, use all the judicial and coercive resources at your command to arrange a confrontation between Esterhazy and Maurice Weil. . . .''

''Maurice Weil? Who is this Maurice Weil?''

He had never heard of him! His surprise turned to astonishment when I told him the improbable story of this Jew.[4]

The public hearings will be resumed tomorrow, when Casimir-Perier and General Mercier are to be heard. The whole town is waiting for the ''bludgeon-stroke.''

I dined and spent the evening with Casimir-Perier.

[4] *Author's note:* See this diary under the date of November 20, 1897.

Colonel Jouaust opened the proceedings at 6:30 A.M.

Casimir-Perier's evidence would have been perfect if it had lacked the suggestion that it was also a personal vindication. He gave a full account of his conversation with Count Münster on January 6, 1895, and this, he said, entitled him to say that the diplomatic incident with Germany had had nothing whatever to do with his resignation.

Finally, in his most trenchant voice, which he was scarcely able to master, he denied the assertions of General Mercier that Lebrun-Renaud had reported to him any confession by Dreyfus.

General Mercier himself followed him at the bar.

The hall was all agog for the dramatic and devastating disclosure which would end the case once and for all. But nothing came, except a commonplace account of the case. Nevertheless, the general told his story with remarkable method, precision, and authority; it took him no less than four-and-a-half hours. His peroration was moving:

"I have not arrived at my age," he said, "without having discovered by sad experience that everything human is fallible. Consequently I have followed with keen anxiety the whole progress of the Dreyfusard campaign. If the slightest doubt had occurred to my mind, gentlemen, I should be the first to tell you so, for I am an honest man, and the son of an honest man. I should come and say to Captain Dreyfus in your presence: 'I made an honest mistake in good faith; I admit it with the same honesty, and I shall do everything humanly possible to make reparation for an appalling error.' But no! The certainty I have felt since 1894 has not undergone the slightest change; it has, indeed, been deepened by a more complete study of the case; and finally it has been fortified by the futility of the efforts made to demonstrate the innocence of the convicted man in spite of the millions of francs that have been spent for the purpose!''

No sooner had he left the platform than Casimir-Perier leaped toward the bar. His eyes flashing, in ringing tones he declared:

''General Mercier has made some statements about my role in 1895 that I do not wish to ratify by silence and cannot allow to pass. I demand to be confronted with him!''

The presiding officer decided that the confrontation should take place on Monday morning.

The court rose at midday.

During the day news reached me from all quarters that General Mercier's interminable speech had left the Nationalists dismayed. What? Was this all he had to say? Not a word about the mysterious and devastating piece of evidence that had been going to end the trial in five minutes? What a disappointment! Meanwhile on the other side there was exultation—premature exultation.

The members of the court made only a brief appearance in the office. Three of them, including Colonel Jouaust, asked me again to show them the documents of January, 1895, but none of them stopped and talked to me. However, Captain Beauvais whispered into General Chamoin's ear:

"A sad morning, sir, which disappointed us greatly!"

Finally, I spent an hour with Casimir-Perier, who wanted to draw on my memory in preparing his reply to General Mercier. When I left him I took the liberty of saying:

"When you are at the bar, I implore you to moderate your voice and produce your arguments quietly."

"Quietly!" he exclaimed. "It's easy for you to say that, my dear fellow, but I've been bottling up what I've got to say for five years while all the time I've been wanting to shriek it to high heaven!"

Sunday, August 13, 1899

Day of rest; I nearly wrote *entr'acte*.

I left early in the morning for St. Malo, from where I went to Dinard to meet Eugène Melchior de Vogüé.

We had a long and intimate talk. I gave him all the impressions of the tragic trial that I have noted in this diary. Vainly we tried to find some explanation for the prisoner's disconcerting psychology. Vogüé urged me to tell him what I expected the outcome of the trial to be. I said to him:

"What strikes me most at present is the effort the members of the court are making to free themselves mentally from their professional discipline, to 'demilitarize' their minds. Will they succeed? To my mind, that is the crux of the matter.... If they had had to give judgment yesterday, under the influence of the violent disappointment caused them by General Mercier's disquisition, I think they would have acquitted Dreyfus, and out of pity rather than conviction. But the trial is only beginning. How will it develop? I am expecting all sorts of surprises and vicissitudes.''

I spent the afternoon alone, wandering along the rocky shore of St. Enogat, in the sweet restfulness of thinking about nothing at all.

Monday, August 14, 1899

At thirty-five minutes past six this morning, immediately after the court had been declared open, there was a loud shout from the end of the hall:

''Labori has just been murdered!''

Tumult immediately arose.

Colonel Jouaust, without losing his calm, ordered silence in court, and then adjourned for half-an-hour at the request of Maître Demange.

I withdrew into the isolated courtyard with the members of the court. A police superintendant soon brought us some news. Labori had been shot in the back, two yards from the house where he is staying in the Place Laënnec; the bullet seemed to have damaged a vertebra. The would-be murderer, a bright young fellow with reddish hair, had run away as fast as his legs would carry him, shouting: ''I've just killed the Dreyfus! I've just killed the Dreyfus!'' and he had van-ished into the country, in the direction of the woods that stretch north of the Vilaine. An immense *battue* of police and *gendarmes*—more than three hundred men —was promptly organized to hunt for him. The whole country is going to be searched. But Du Halgouët, who is a Breton to the core, and has lived long in the area, said to me with a proud smile:

"The *gendarmes* and the police will come back empty-handed, for the attempted murderer will have the whole population on his side. I know our peasants. They never denounce each other, any more than they ever agree to give evidence against each other. They have remained exactly as they were at the time of the *chouannerie.*" [5]

At fifteen minutes past seven the court proceedings were resumed with the confrontation of Casimir-Perier and General Mercier. The encounter was painful to listen to. Casimir-Perier spoke loudly and trenchantly —but clumsily; his opponent spoke with cold, poisonous—and cruel—impertinence. As for the subject-matter of their dispute, the general vigorously maintained his assertions about the "night of anxiety," the "tragic night" of January 6, 1895.

"That night," he said, "the Prime Minister and I remained until half-past twelve in the office of the President of the Republic, waiting for the result of the exchange of telegrams between the Kaiser and Count Münster, waiting to know whether the outcome of the crisis was to be peace or war."

After all the documents I had shown them, the mem-

[5] Militant rising of Breton Royalists in 1793.

bers of the court seemed dumfounded by these solemn and obstinate assertions.

As soon as the court adjourned, they surrounded me and pressed me with questions. Once again I assured them that nothing whatever had happened on the evening of January 6, 1895, for the excellent reason that the incident had been closed since three o'clock in the afternoon. I added:

"After all, if there had been any danger of war between Germany and France, how is it that the Commander-in-Chief, General Saussier, was given no warning? Perhaps he would have had something to say in such circumstances. Now, I have it from his own lips that at that period he never for one moment envisaged the possibility of mobilization." [6]

"All the same, General Mercier is not mad!" Captain Parfait objected, with pursed lips.

"Certainly he is not, nor is he a liar. But I think he is unconsciously suffering from an illusion of memory, the strange complaint called restrospective auto-suggestion."

Hanotaux, the next witness, confirmed the members of the court in the idea that something was being withheld from them, for he evaded all questions about his conversations with the German Ambassador.

"On that," he said, "I can only refer you to the diplomatic file, particularly as it has been submitted to you complete."

With Generals Billot, Chanoine, and Zurlinden, all former Ministers of War, it was a different matter.

[6] *Author's note:* See this diary under date January 13, 1895.

They evaded no questions. Holding their heads high, they declared their respect for the *res judicata* and well *judicata,* their complete confidence in the evidence accumulated by the intelligence department, their unshakable conviction that the author of the *bordereau,* the German agent, the supplier of information to Schwartzkoppen, was Dreyfus.

Next came Cavaignac, his body emaciated, a gleam in his deep-set eyes, his skin greenish, as if impregnated with bile. He went back to the beginning of the case and delivered a powerful summary of the whole of the General Staff case. His imperious mask, his dogmatic self-assurance, the severity of his demeanor, gave him the air of an inquisitor addressing the Holy Office *de pravitate judaíca.* The members of the court listened in fascination; I could feel his indictment biting into their minds like acid eating into a copper plate.

Dreyfus filled me with compassion. Pale, dismayed, and his mouth agape, he listened in gloomy stupefaction to this irrefutable demonstration of his guilt. At one moment his eyes glazed, a pearl of sweat appeared at his temples, his whole face expressed a most appalling distress. He seemed to say: "Do what you like with me; I can stand it no longer!"

Chamoin, who is a sensitive person, leaned toward me.

"Look at him! What a martyr!" he said. "They'll acquit him, even if only out of pity!"

But on the way out of the courtroom, I overheard this scrap of conversation between Major Merle and Major Profillet:

"That was a fine speech of Cavaignac's, wasn't it?"
"Yes, and we can see clearly now!"

The day ended without Labori's assailant's having
been found; the *gendarmes* and police came back
empty-handed, as Du Halgouët had foreseen.

Rennes was in a turmoil. At first the Nationalists
were crestfallen, for trying to kill a lawyer who is
about to do his duty is a crime that lacks elegance. But
in their rage the Dreyfusards committed the stupidity
of attributing to their opponents collectively an absurd and disgraceful deed that could have been conceived only in the mind of a monomaniac. They went
about proclaiming everywhere: "Murderers! Murderers! General staff of criminals! In future we shall
take hostages. For everyone of ours we shall kill
one of theirs, Mercier, Cavaignac, Boisdeffre, Barrès,
Judet!" Sometimes an angry voice even shouted:
"Down with the generals! Down with the army!" At
this the Nationalists raised their heads and showed
their teeth.

The prefect, the mayor, the deputies, the cardinal-
archbishop made tremendous efforts to allay all these
extravagances. Moreover parties of infantrymen and
gunners are patrolling the town in all directions. Dragoons from Dinard are to arrive this evening.

Tuesday, August 15, 1899

Another *entr'acte,* for the festival of the Assumption.

At mass the priest chanted the sublime and prophetic
verses of the Psalmist: *Propter veritatem, mansuetu-*

*dinem et justitiam, deducet te mirabiliter dextra tua.
Audi, filia, et vide, et inclina aurem tuam, quia con-
cupivit Rex speciem . . . Alleluia!* "Because of truth
and meekness and righteousness, thy right hand shall
teach thee marvelous things. Hearken, O daughter, and
consider, and incline thine ear; so shall the King
greatly desire thy beauty. . . . Amen."

Truth, meekness, and righteousness are the things
most lacking in this terrible trial; and I very much fear
that marvels will not be accomplished.

I took advantage of the holiday to make a pilgrimage
to Combourg, which is twenty-five miles from Rennes
on the St. Malo road.

I had been there twice before, some years ago, in the
first fervor of my romanticism, when the charms and
philters of the "enchanter" stirred me delightfully.
Today I soon realized that I should have done better
not to come. The tall, feudal tower, the fine park, the
poetical pond, even the charming shadows of the sylph-
hide, Lucile and Velléda, left me cold; for the odious
phantoms of Rennes relentlessly occupied my mind.

On the way back I wondered what Chateaubriand
would have thought of the Dreyfus case. I imagine that
the legal riddle would not have interested him, but that
he would have felt better than anybody the symbolic
grandeur and somber lyricism of this drama, one of the
most poignant by which the French conscience has ever
been rent. What would have been his worldly attitude?
Would he have sided with the Dreyfusards or the Nationalists? I imagine that the former Coblentz *émigré*
and soldier of the "princes' army" could only have

been hostile to the Jew's cause. But Chateaubriand, the vindictive and disillusioned Royalist, the bitter pamphleteer of 1825, who denounced the universal "conspiracy of hypocrisy and stupidity," would not have resisted the temptation of shocking the "noble quarter" by declaring himself a Dreyfusard. Also, perhaps, the great literary advocate of Christianity would have found it more beautiful, more poetic, to be on the victim's side. Moreover, I do not recall that he ever spoke of the Jews with animosity. Finally, like a certain Catholic writer of our time, he was susceptible to the charm of Jewesses.[7]

Wednesday, August 16, 1899

The first hour in court today was taken up with consideration of the measures of constraint and confinement to which Dreyfus was subjected during his five years on Devil's Island. In comparison with his atrocious treatment, the system in the Russian convict pris-

---

[7] *Author's note:* He once said to Fontanes: "Jewesses have escaped from the curse of their race. None of them were to be found in the crowd that insulted the Son of Man, whipped Him, crowned Him with thorns, made Him submit to the disgrace and agony of the cross. The women of Judaea believed in the Savior, loved Him, followed Him, and ministered unto Him. A woman of Bethany poured the precious nard on His head; the woman who was a sinner poured oil on His feet; the daughters of Jerusalem wept over Him; the Holy Women accompanied Him to Calvary, bought balms and spices, and then sought Him at the sepulcher, weeping. *Mulier, quid ploras?* . . . The reflection of some beautiful ray will have rested on the forehead of Jewesses." He adds naively: "M. de Fontanes appeared satisfied with this explanation."—*Essai sur la littérature anglaise,* V, 764.

ons as described to us by Dostoevski in *The House of the Dead* or Kropotkin in his *Memories of a Prisoner of State* seem the gentlest, the most charitable, the most civilized form that the vindication of society could take. It made the most painful impression on the public; heads were lowered even among the witnesses for the prosecution. During this long reminder of his tortures, the prisoner did not once speak. At the end, when Colonel Jouaust asked him if he had anything to say he replied coldly:

"I am not here to talk about the abominable tortures to which I have been subjected; I shall speak only to defend my honor."

After this incident the sergeant-usher brought in Mme Henry. Tall, slender, and dark, with fine eyes which shone beneath her long crêpe veils, she very agreeably filled the role of "our national Artemis," as the militarist newspapers call her, or, better still, "the tragic widow of our new D'Assas." I do not think she has changed since the first time I saw her in the spring of 1897 on the Esplanade des Invalides, walking with her husband and Lauth.

While she raised her veils slightly to take the oath, the thought struck me that the whole secret of the Dreyfus case lay behind that narrow brow, beneath that head of wavy hair. But would she speak?

She was questioned about the circumstances in which Henry received the *bordereau,* and answered evasively, in unfinished sentences. Lieutenant-Colonel Brongniart then asked:

"When your husband wrote to you on the day of his

death: 'You know in whose interest I acted,' to whom
was he referring?''

For a moment she shut her eyes. Then, in a hesitat-
ing, sing-song voice, like a little girl reciting her cate-
chism, she said:

"It was in the interest of the army ... the army that
my dear husband committed . . . committed his crime.
It was the interest of the army that always guided . . .
guided his conduct. And in the interest of whom else,
gentlemen, could you believe that he would act?''

Brongniart insisted with his question. She repeated
in the identical words:

"It was in the interest of the army that my dear husband. . . .''

Colonel Jouaust, in a discouraged voice, gave her
permission to withdraw. When she walked down the
steps from the platform, Major Lauth offered her his
arm and escorted her to the door. It was a suggestive
picture.

The court had now been sitting for two hours and a
half, and granted itself a twenty-minute adjournment.
Lieutenant-Colonel Brongniart came over to me in the
yard.

"It was dreadful! She wouldn't say anything! Will
you be in the office later? I shall come and see you.''

When the court resumed, the next witness was General Roget, formerly principal private secretary to
Cavaignac.

With his very first words he established an ascend-
ancy over the members of the court. His martial figure,
his crisp phrases, his loud voice, quickly put them all

under his thumb; he might have been ordering them to carry out a maneuver. If the court had had to bring in its verdict there and then, Dreyfus would once more have been unanimously found guilty.

When Lieutenant-Colonel Brongniart came to see me this afternoon, I was struck by his gloomy expression. After deploring Mme Henry's reluctance to speak he said:

"Now we know all about the case that is ascertainable from our own resources. The only additional source of information is the Kaiser."

"And if such information were offered to you, how would you take it?"

"With gratitude," he replied, without hesitation.

No sooner had he left than Captain Beauvais and Captain Parfait opened the door. They were red-cheeked and looked lively and in high spirits, having just come back from a long ride on horseback.

"We're not disturbing you, are we?" they asked me cheerfully.

"Certainly not!"

"It wouldn't bore you to talk to us a little?"

"On the contrary, I should be delighted."

I offered them chairs and cigarettes, and then I took from the drawer a bottle of port, from which I filled three glasses, to the astonishment of three military prisoners who were sadly sweeping the yard outside the bars of my open window.

"It seems," Beauvais said "that you have astonishing pipelines leading to Esterhazy and Weil; Lieutenant-Colonel Brongniart suggested we should come along and talk to you about them.''

I told them what I told Brongniart the other day— the fantastic story of those two scoundrels who, with impunity, have combined swindling with treason for so many years.

My visitors seemed to enjoy my story greatly. But from certain remarks that they let slip I could tell that it in no way modified their view of Dreyfus' guilt; for this very morning General Roget super-abundantly demonstrated to them that Esterhazy was not the author of the *bordereau,* and that the disorders of his private life, however appalling they might be, had no possible connection with the crime of 1894.

Perhaps an even graver symptom of their inner thought was that Parfait, backed up by Beauvais, said to me:

"Did you read the open letter to General Mercier in the *Gaulois* of the day before yesterday?"

"Yes. It was reproduced in most of the newspapers."

"Weren't you impressed by it?"

"Not in the least! It was a new version of the 'tragic night' story, and you know what I think of that! All the same, the letter in the *Gaulois* has one advantage; it calls on General Mercier to speak out frankly about the document said to have been annotated by the Kaiser and photographed by the War Ministry before being restored to him. The letter says: 'You possess a copy of that photograph, general, and you brought it with you to Rennes. If our information, for which we have very good authority, is correct, confirm it; if it is false, deny it.' Why do you not put the question to General Mercier?''

Beauvais and Parfait looked at each other for a moment. Then they muttered something vague, and left me, after a hearty handshake.

Thursday, August 17, 1890

General Roget ended his overwhelming evidence.

Then, after a pathetic confrontation between Mme Henry and the magistrate Bertulus, a fawning, equivocal, furtive, and nebulous character whom it would not be surprising to meet in a ''Tale of Hoffman,'' the sergeant-usher brought in the next witness, ''M.'' Picquart.

The former chief of the intelligence service expressed himself with ease, clarity, and logic, but he ignored rather too much the principal rule of military eloquence, which, according to Cicero, is *rem contrahere,* the art of conciseness. Also he made it too evident that he was speaking *pro domo sua.*

All the time that he was at the bar, he reminded me of an heresiarch, an apostate, appearing before an ecclesiastic court. Anxious to rehabilitate himself in the eyes of his peers, he seemed, nevertheless, to mistrust them, to be speaking over their heads to the public, to ''impartial posterity.'' Hence the abrupt alternations in his voice between submission and revolt.

Moreover, he was obviously embarrassed and disconcerted, as it were, by the fact that he was appearing in civilian—I nearly said ''lay''—clothes before his former comrades in full dress uniform.

Toward the end of the day, walking with Du Halgouët in the old streets that surround the church of St. Étienne, I saw Major de Bréon entering the porch of the ancient Augustine chapel.

I knew him to be a man of great piety, very rigorous in his devotions. One of his brothers had entered the priesthood. Du Halgouët said to me:

"My family knows the Bréons very well. They are very fine people, very Catholic. . . . Every morning and every night the major spends a long time in prayer, praying to God to reveal to him whether Dreyfus is guilty or not; and, as no light has come, at any rate so far, he is terribly distressed."

"That does not surprise me. Anxiety and distress are written on his face."

If Major de Bréon's conscience is tormented by doubts, I believe Major Merle's conscience to be perfectly serene. He does not spend hours in prayer, and I am sure that since the trial began he has not lost a minute's sleep or a mouthful of food. Not once has he asked a question, opened a file, taken a note. He takes part in the court proceedings as he would in a review, his head erect, his eyes fixed—and vacant. He is not a judge, but a saber. I imagine that the Duc d'Enghien must have seen some faces like that among General Hulin's assessors.

Friday, August 18, 1899

Picquart's evidence went on for another five hours! It ended with his confrontation with General Mercier and General Roget.

The acrimonious and brutal tone in which the two generals spoke betrayed the extent of the hatred roused by "M." Picquart among his former comrades. A strange thing that I have often noticed is that Dreyfus is not an object of hatred among army officers. They talk about him with stern coldness or contempt, but without anger, and sometimes even with pity. But the mere mention of the name of Picquart rouses them; they hate, loathe, and execrate the renegade to the point of frenzy.

On the way out of court, when I saw Dreyfus surrounded by the *gendarmes* who were taking him back to the military prison, the physical state to which he was reduced reminded me of Heine's remark that, "Judaism is not a religion; it is a misfortune."

Saturday, August 19, 1899

General de Boisdeffre was called.

He has been on the unemployed list for a year, since the dreadful day when he was broken by the discovery of the "Henry forgery." Since then he has aged a great deal; his figure, formerly so straight and elegant, is bent. His appearance and movements suggest a man of sixty-five; he is only sixty.

In his evidence he recapitulated the whole General Staff case and concluded:

"I said in 1894 that I regarded the case against Captain Dreyfus as proved. My certainty of his guilt is no less strong today."

Positive though these words were, his voice was flat

and tired and sounded broken. I do not doubt his good faith, as he was speaking under oath, but all the same I should like to know what is happening in the recesses of his mind, in the obscure region where conversions take place, as well as the mysterious workings of grace.

He was followed by General Gonse, who hemmed and hawed, hesitated, floundered, said things, and withdrew them. I do not know which predominated in his disconcerting evidence, dim-wittedness or sincerity, dissimulation or stupidity. How well he summed himself up a few months ago when he said to me: "In short, I am either the worst of wretches or the worst of fools!" [8]

Sunday, August 20, 1899

I had lunch at Dinard, in the handsome villa which the department of Ile-et-Vilaine puts at the disposal of its prefect. It overlooks the emerald port and has an immense view stretching from Cap Fréhel to the headland of Grand-Bé.

The light was vibrant and crystalline, and the waves broke serenely and rhythmically on the shore. Under the radiant sky the sea, like watered silk, shimmered into the distance until it disappeared from sight.

Our lunch was very gay. General Chamoin and Viguié, the director of the Sûreté Générale, were among the guests. We all felt the same relief at escaping from our troubles at Rennes.

Viguié told me about the fruitless efforts he had lav-

[8] General Gonse was relieved of his post on July 29, 1898 and put on the reserve on September 19, 1903. He died in 1907.

ished in all directions to track down the would-be murderer of Labori.

"I could mention many people who saw him running away, recognized him, spoke to him, and even gave him shelter," he said. "Well, not one of them would tell us his name; they all evaded our inquiries. I understand now why the Convention, the Directory, and the Consulate had so much difficulty in putting down the *chouannerie*.

"And at that time they had a very effective method of getting the peasants to talk: slowly roasting the soles of their feet."

"Ah! those were good times . . . for the police!"

Monday, August 21, 1899

General Fabre and Colonel d'Aboville gave evidence this morning. They were followed by the officers of the information department: Major Lauth, Captain Junck, and the archivist Gribelin.

When "M." Picquart was before the court a few days ago, he seemed to me to typify the figure of the heresiarch; Major Lauth seems to me to typify the impostor.

He sustained his role admirably. He picked his way through his lies with masterly nimbleness, self-assurance, and dexterity. It is to him above all to whom there should be applied the mysterious sentence with which Henry ended his last letter to his wife: "You know in *whose* interest I acted."

When the court adjourned, the members of the court

did not conceal from me their admiration of the excellent statement they had just heard. Lieutenant-Colonel Brongniart, who no doubt noticed my reserve, said to me:

"Do you know Lauth well?"

I answered coldly:

"He is the only officer of the General Staff with whom I have broken off all relations."

Brongniart left it at that.

What a curious picture Rennes presents, and what a field for moral observations!

The leading spirit, the great puller of strings on the Nationalist side is General Mercier. He has installed himself in a modest house that belongs to his old friend, the retired General de Saint-Germain. Here the supporters of the army gather every afternoon and evening; first of all the crowd of military witnesses, then Cavaignac, Jules Lemaître, Maurice Barrès, Drumont, Auffray, Villebois-Mareuil, Judet, Maizières, Max Régis, and finally the squireens of provincial Brittany and many ecclesiastics. It is from here that watchwords are issued and next day's evidence is worked out and concerted. General Mercier causes rigorous discipline to prevail throughout the camp.

How different is the situation in the opposite camp! At least a dozen groups, coteries, and camarillas are continually forming, dissolving, and quarreling, spying on, congratulating, and excommunicating each other. So far as I can make them out, there are the clear-headed, the doctrinaires, the intellectuals, the enthusiasts, the radicals, the socialists, the anti-militarist ranters, the stateless persons. I mention a few names at random, more or less in that ascending scale: Molinier, Cornély, Paul Meyer, André Chevrillon, Gabriel Monod, Giry, Marcel Prévost, Jules Claretie, Reclus, Louis Havet, Psichari, Octave Mirbeau, Ranc, Victor Basch, Viviani, Jaurès, Leyman, Séverine, Cohen, Ader, etc. I nearly forgot—which would be an injustice to Dreyfus—a large number of foreigners—English, German, Italian, Russian, Belgian, Dutch, Scandinavian, Swiss, and American—most of whom are of the Jewish type.

In these overheated circles, which are haunted by but a single thought, the maddest rumors gain credence with incredible rapidity, and minds are intoxicated and hypnotized by mutual suggestion. I can understand what collective psychoses were like in the old days, the great psychological epidemics that gave rise to the flagellants, the Illuminati, the convulsionaries, etc.

Tuesday, August 22, 1899

Maître Labori, convalescent but still quite stiff in his joints, reappeared on the defense bench. Colonel Jouaust welcomed him with a few simple and worthy words. He replied with swollen phrases and melodramatic gestures, the kind of eloquence least suited to a military audience.

Evidence was given by Lieutenant-Colonel Bertin-Mourot, Major Rollin, Lieutenant-Colonel Gendron, etc. The intelligence department was exposed to the disturbing light of day. It was a sad spectacle.

This afternoon Lieutenant-Colonel Brongniart, Major de Bréon, and Major Profillet bewailed in my presence their inability to see light about the crime of 1894, and they asked me "if there were not some way of getting Germany to submit to us, or at any rate to publish, the documents enumerated in the *bordereau*." I replied:

"There is only one *honorable* way: to send a rogatory commission to take evidence from Colonel von Schwartzkoppen. But I doubt whether his chiefs would give him permission to appear before it. As for a diplomatic *démarche* in Berlin, do not count on it. M. Delcassé would certainly not consent to apply for German aid in a trial that is solely under French jurisdiction."

All three looked at each other in silence; then they withdrew, looking very grave.

While I was finishing a letter to Delcassé giving him an account of this conversation, Maître Demange came in. He wanted to check the date of certain events that had been in dispute during the morning. When he had finished taking his notes he got up, hesitantly. Then with an anxious air and a broken voice, he said to me:

"I am on the right road, am I not? Dreyfus is innocent? You do not doubt it?"

"No, I do not doubt it."

"Thank you, thank you. . . . One more question, if you will permit me. We have heard from Paris that in your telegrams to M. Delcassé you forsee a conviction."

"Excuse me if I do not answer that."

Wednesday, August 23, 1899

After the hearing of some secondary witnesses, the clerk read a transcription of the evidence given by Esterhazy to the Criminal Chamber on January 23, 24, and 30 last, because he now refuses to leave London, though he does not cease to send his startled former patrons letters such as this:

> *A tough customer such as myself must not be driven to despair. . . . When I produce what I have to say they will all be done for. Oh! the scoundrels. . . . Done for though I may be, on the day I wish it there will be two big leaders who will not escape their punishment. Oh! the brutes! . . . . When you see General Gonse, tell him on my behalf that he will end his life in jail. . . . I shall not die alone, and I assure you that I shall arrange myself a fine funeral. . . .*

The tough customer's statements in the Criminal Chamber provided Maître Labori with a wonderful opportunity to fulminate against General Gonse and General de Boisdeffre. This was not legal argument; it was battle. If he goes on in this tone, perhaps he will win his case in the eyes of public opinion, but he will certainly lose it before the court-martial.

For some days past, I have noticed a detail which may appear insignificant in itself, but cannot fail to affect the minds of the members of the court because of the association of ideas to which it leads. During the hearings Picquart sits at the extreme left of the central block of seats, noticeably apart from the other military witnesses who, being witnesses for the prosecution, all sit together to the right of the central block, behind the bigwigs. Near him, but on the other side of the balustrade that supports the back of his bench, is the regular seat of the Socialist leaders, Jaurès, Viviani, etc. Between them and the "unfrocked hero" there takes place a continual interchange of rapid remarks, which, it can be guessed, are alternately denigratory, sarcastic, or disgusted. This picturesque grouping of three is only too symbolic; it looks like a photograph of the often denounced alliance between Dreyfusism and statelessness, between the defenders of the Jew and the destroyers of our national traditions. I fear that the Jew will pay for this edifying spectacle.

At about five o'clock there was a timid knock on my office door. It was General de Boisdeffre.

He collapsed rather than sat on the chair that Du Halgouët offered him. His emaciated features, his dejected appearance, the big yellow lines which furrowed his brow, his whole look of suffering, filled me with such pity that I said:

"What is the matter, general? Are you ill?"

"No, I am not ill, but I am suffering greatly. . . . This morning's hearing. . . . What agony! What an abomination!"

His voice choked, and his eyes filled with tears. Du Halgouët made as if to go out, but Boisdeffre told him to stay. Then, pulling himself together a little, he went on.

"I have confidence in you two," he said. "I am sure

that neither of you will abuse my trust. I have come to you on an absolutely personal and private matter, which is on my conscience. . . . This, my dear Paléologue, is what I want to ask you. Why did Henry . . . and others as well, perhaps, commit all these aberrations, since there is no doubt about Dreyfus' guilt?''

''That is easy to answer. I have only to put your question the other way about. Why should Henry and *certainly* others as well have committed all these aberrations if they had not felt that you and General Gonse were going to be forced to acknowledge Dreyfus' innocence?''

He passed his hand across his brow, and murmured:

''Good heavens! Good heavens! . . . But what has happened? . . . What do you know?''

''I *know* nothing. If I did, I should have stated it before the Cour de Cassation. But, by way of hypotheses and cross-checking, I have come to be convinced of Dreyfus' innocence.''

''Then you believe the guilty man is Esterhazy?''

''I believe that the guilty *men* are Esterhazy, Weil, Henry, and a fourth individual about whom nobody has yet thought.''

He remained prostrate, with haggard eyes.

''I understand less and less, for I can neither accept your opinion nor refute it. . . . But there's nothing left for me but to disappear. I'm finished, finished!''

I tried to cheer him with some friendly words, and then I touched the sensitive chord.

''General,'' I said, ''I shall not let you go without telling you the one thing most likely to comfort you.

M. Delcassé's recent mission to St. Petersburg was a complete success. I do not yet know any details because I have not seen the Minister since his return. But he had me informed by his principal private secretary that the case made in my memorandum No. 2 prevailed.''

I explained to General de Boisdeffre the substance of that memorandum and the lines along which it conceived the future development of the Franco-Russian alliance.

His face relaxed and his equanimity was suddenly restored.

"What a lot of good you have done me!" he exclaimed. "You have reminded me of something we should never forget! Above us, beyond us, there is always France, eternal France!... *Vive la France!*"

I had put him back again into his soldier's shell. But for how long had I rescued him from his bitter thoughts?

Thursday, August 24, 1899

A stormy sitting; the chief point at issue was a secret file submitted to the 1894 court-martial. Now according to the evidence of Captain Freystoetter, who was a member of that court, a falsified version of the Panizzardi telegram had been put into that file, to say nothing of other documents that had nothing to do with Dreyfus.

In the discussion on this ticklish subject Maître Labori again distinguished himself by his aggressive behavior, his impetuous gestures, his violent and dramatic dialectics. His very wise and subtle colleague, Maître Demange, listened to him in alarm.

Friday, August 25, 1899

The handwriting experts, including the famous Bertillon, chief of the criminal records office at the prefecture of police, gave their interminable evidence.

Bertillon, who is ingenious, learned, and completely honest, is certainly not in full possession of his faculties. His whole argument is nothing but a long tissue of absurdities deduced from each other, entangled with each other, and confirming each other. Moreover, his vocabulary seems to derive from a book of thaumaturgic spells; and finally, his moonstruck eyes, his sepulchral voice, the saturnine magnetism that he exudes, create the impression that one is in the presence of a necromancer.

The members of the court, all of whom bear the mental imprint of the École Polytechnique,[9] were captivated, if not fascinated, by his vast display of scientific learning and listened to him in religious awe. Officers who came from St. Cyr or from the ranks listened in less docile fashion.

While Bertillon was performing his hocus-pocus and displaying his phantasmagorial drawings, I wondered whether it was not possible that this semi-maniac might not unknowingly have hit on one of the general laws to which all handwriting is subject, the automa-

[9] Military academy of artillery and engineering.

tism of certain rhythms, for instance; on this foundation of positive truth, his crazy imagination would
give itself full rein—just like a fifteenth-century astrol-
oger who in his apocalyptic meditations might have
had a vague premonition of Kepler's laws and used it
as a basis for his horoscopes.[10]

To recover from this exhausting sitting, from which
I emerged with my brain reeling, I walked up and down
the little flower garden outside the court office with
Carrière. The worthy major, with a jovial air, pipe in
mouth, playing with his dog and crow, told me some
side-splitting barrack-room and garrison stories. Then,
delighted at the pleasure he was giving me, he told me
that he had a lot of still better stories in store for me.

"But it's not I that shall tell you them," he said.
"Just wait a moment!"

He went up to the iron door that gave access to the
interior of the prison, pushed back the bolt of the
wicket-gate, and called the sergeant-porter. The latter
was a fine, soldierly figure.

[10] On April 18, 1905, the Cour de Cassation, having reopened its
inquiry into the Dreyfus case, submitted Bertillon's findings to three
experts, nominated by the Academy of Science. These were Darboux,
the permanent secretary of the academy, and Appell and Henri
Poincaré, both members of the Institut de France and professors
of mathematics in the Paris faculty. In a unanimous report the three
experts said: "The system used by Bertillon is devoid of all scientific
value (1) because the rules for the calculation of probabilities were
not correctly observed; (2) because his work is the result of a com-
plex treatment inflicted upon the original document from which the
latter emerged corrupted, having been subjected to a series of photographic enlargements and reductions, and even to tracing, retracing,
cutting, pasting up, whiting over, brushing over, and retouching."

"Come here a moment!" Carrière called out to him cheerfully. "Tell us your stories, and the best ones!"

The old N.C.O., with the utmost naturalness and simplicity and in a most likable manner, started telling me his life-story. . . . It was appalling!

He had started as a sergeant in the disciplinary companies and military penal establishments in southern Algeria, after which he had been appointed a supervisor of transportation to Guiana, *i.e.*, a warder. As he was known for his energy, he had always been chosen for the toughest jobs, *e.g.*, at the Île Royale prison, where the most dangerous convicts are confined, or the Maroni hard labor camps, where the most rebellious wills are eventually broken. Now, on the eve of his retirement, he was spending his last days of service in the pleasant prison of Rennes. But against the background of this career, which has such fine moral unity, what amusing experiences he had had! The good Major Carrière made the worthy man unlock all his memories for my benefit—escapes, revolts, executions, beatings, hanging by the legs; and since we are in the country of Chateaubriand, I wish to say to the old warder: "Son of Lasthenes, thy tale delights me!"

Colonel Jouaust appeared and called me.

"Have you heard the news that the Nationalist newspapers claim to have received from Brussels, 'The truth revealed by a Russian diplomatist'?" he said.

"Yes, I was informed of it last night from Paris; it's so absurd that I didn't dare mention it to you."

The so-called "Russian diplomatist" has revived on his own account the myth of "the document annotated in the Kaiser's own hand, a copy of which is in General Mercier's possession." The former War Minister being determined to produce this vital document at the Rennes court-martial, he said, the Government of the French Republic had thought it necessary to send M. Delcassé to St. Petersburg to find out what the attitude of Russia would be if war became inevitable. "The Czar personally assured M. Delcassé that France could count on the support of the Russian armies; he insisted, however, that General Mercier should be warned that, if his disclosures provoked a conflict with Germany, he would be immediately arrested." I said to Colonel Jouaust:

"Have I any need to deny this arrant nonsense?"

"Yes; I need your denial for other persons."

With these only too significant words, he left me.

At midnight I was handed a telegram from Delcassé urgently summoning me to Paris. I am taking the seven-thirty train tomorrow morning.

Saturday, August 26, 1899

Delcassé received me at four o'clock. The substance of what he said to me was this:

(1) I entirely approve of your attitude at Rennes and your personal relations with the members of the court.

(2) I am grateful for the spontaneous answer you gave to members of the court that the Republican Government could not intervene in Berlin to ask for the restoration of documents delivered in 1894.

(3) Should any documents be offered me by a foreign power, I do not see that I should have any right to refuse them. But on no pretext whatever shall I condescend to ask Germany or Italy to help us to solve a judicial problem which comes solely under French authority.

(4) If documents were submitted to us by a foreign power, they could be submitted to the court only *in camera* by you.

(5) According to a telegram just decoded by our deciphering service, Tornielli, the Italian Ambassador, is trying to persuade his Government that it should submit to us documents delivered by Esterhazy.

In conclusion Delcassé said to me:

"You still believe that Dreyfus is going to be convicted?"

"Yes, unless there is some dramatic *coup de théâtre,* which can now come only from Rome or Berlin, and seems unlikely to me."

The Minister gave me an appointment for nine-thirty tomorrow morning, to talk to me about his trip to St. Petersburg.

Sunday, August 27, 1899

I went to Delcassé's at half-past nine. He told me about his visit to St. Petersburg and his conversations with the Czar and with Muraviev, and described the negotiations in detail. By the terms of letters exchanged between the two Foreign Ministers on July 28 and August 9, the military convention of 1892, which was

tied to the existence of the Triple Alliance, will be
coterminous with the diplomatic agreement by which
France and Russia bound themselves "for the safe-
guarding of their common and *permanent* interests";
in other words, it would remain in force even if the
Triple Alliance were dissolved. Delcassé, with a flash
in his eyes, concluded:

"And now we must detach Italy from the Triple
Alliance!"

After he had finished, he said:

"Do you have to be back at Rennes tomorrow morning?"

"No. The hearing will be entirely devoted to the
handwriting experts' reports; there will certainly be
no cause for me to intervene."

"Then this is what I should like you to do. Take
home my St. Petersburg file and write me a detailed
memorandum on my mission, making use of what I
have just told you. Bring it to me tomorrow morning,
before you leave for Rennes."

Monday, August 28, 1899

I had a brief talk with Delcassé at eight o'clock this
morning, when I handed him my memorandum on his
mission to St. Petersburg.

Immediately afterward I took the train to Rennes,
where I arrived at four o'clock.

This morning's sitting was not marked by any incident; it was exclusively devoted to the reports of the
handwriting experts.

This morning's sitting was one of the saddest that I have yet attended. Once more all the intelligence department's dirty linen was displayed in public. The former deputy chief of the service, Lieutenant-Colonel Cordier, who was Sandherr's close collaborator and has now retired, is a recent convert to Dreyfusism, and this has unleashed the fury of the General Staff against him. However, the "renegade's" disclosures were of no effect because he produced them in a thick, mumbling voice, a rambling manner, with comic gestures, tremulous hands, and vacant eyes, and, finally, smelled intolerably of absinthe from a distance of twenty paces. When he appeared before the Criminal Chamber last December, he had to be asked to come back another day because he was drunk when he appeared in court.

The members of the court-martial were too discreet to question me about my journey to Paris. But I learned from General Chamoin how curious they were about it. So during an adjournment, I said to Lieutenant-Colonel Brongniart:

"I mentioned confidentially to M. Delcassé the concern that I observed was felt by a number of persons here about documents that accompanied the *bordereau* and are said to be in Berlin. He told me in the most positive manner that he would not consent under any pretext whatever to ask the Imperial Government for the restitution of those documents."

Brongniart thanked me with a disappointed air.

Wednesday, August 30, 1899

Three experts, three very learned men—Paul Meyer, professor at the Collège de France, Molinier, professor at the École des Chartes, and Giry, professor at the École des Hautes-Études—set out to prove incontrovertibly that the handwriting of the *bordereau* was Esterhazy's.

The court listened to them with scrupulous but mistrustful attention, for it regards them primarily as "intellectuals," presumptuous pedants and members of a caste who believe that they constitute an aristocracy of the intellect and are all more or less lost to patriotism.

At about three o'clock Lieutenant-Colonel Brongniart and Major de Bréon came to see me in the court office.

"If Germany declared herself ready to let us have the documents enumerated in the *bordereau*, what would M. Delcassé do?" they asked.

"I am sure that he would agree, and that he would instruct me to submit them to you *in camera*. But I do not believe that Germany has any intention of offering them to us."

They both looked at me in consternation. To enlighten them about the state of mind prevalent in Berlin, I read them two extracts from the semi-official *Cologne Gazette,* dated August 16 and 29. The first of these said:

If after the statements made by the German Government and the proceedings in the Cour de Cassation, there is anyone who still believes that Dreyfus is guilty, all one can say is that he is either suffering from mental illness or desires deliberately the conviction of an innocent man. One is helpless in relation to such persons, and nothing that the German Government could publish would make any impression on them. The documents supplied by us would be declared to be false; and from the fact that Germany was trying to save Dreyfus the conclusion would be drawn that he was our spy.

The tone of the second extract was even more abrupt. It was as follows:

Numerous efforts are made to move the German Government and persuade Colonel Schwartzkoppen to drop his reserve. When one sees what credit is given in France to the statements of Colonel Panizzardi, one is forced to conclude that Colonel Schwartzkoppen's evidence would not possess the gift of convincing people who do not want to be convinced. Germany has done her duty and more than her duty. When the Chancellor speaks as Count von Bülow has spoken, he speaks in the name of the Empire and the Emperor, and there can be no question but that he speaks the truth. If there are persons in France for whom all this amounts to nothing, it only dishonors their character and discredits their good sense. Germany cannot support the solemn declarations she has already made with any written evidence or any new testimony.

"Obviously we can no longer expect any light from Germany," Brongniart said.

A few moments later I repeated all this to Colonel Jouaust, who listened with contracted features.

Thursday, August 31, 1899

This morning's hearing, which was almost entirely *in camera,* provided curious evidence of the military mentality. The question at issue was whether Dreyfus, by reason of his rank and his employment, could in 1894 have been familiar with the secret mechanism of the "120 short" gun, more particularly its "hydropneumatic buffer." Major Hartmann, who served for a long time in the arsenal at Bourges, declared that there was no way by which an ordinary captain on the General Staff could procure information about it, because the actual arrangements for its manufacture were carefully concealed. This was denied by General Deloye, the director of artillery at the Ministry of War.

If there was ever a subject which should have been discussed calmly, it was this, because it was exclusively concerned with mechanical processes, systems of levers, gears, pistons, etc. In fact, however, the proceedings were stormy and agitated because they set at loggerheads officers of unequal rank.

The discussion grew embittered at the first few words; it was not just a technical disagreement, but a battle between a superior and a subordinate, a major opposing a major-general.

From the strictly disciplinary point of view, Hartmann's words and manner were irreproachable. But his independence of judgment, the obstinacy with which he maintained his arguments, the intractability with which he declined to accept the official hierarchical truth, and perhaps also some stiffness in his attitude, completely alienated the members of the court. Every now and then they cast angry glances at him, as if he were a disciple of Picquart's or himself a Picquart at the beginning of his apostasy, over whom excommunication already hovered. *Si quis negaverit, anathema sit.*

Friday, September 1, 1899

The eighteenth day of this interminable trial. It was devoted to hearing secondary witnesses.

I have seen nothing sadder since I have been at Rennes than the procession of Dreyfus' old friends, or rather his old comrades; for even in the days of his prosperity he never had a friend. All of them in giving evidence against him seem to be spitting in his face; and it is a heartbreaking sight to see them recalling the happy confidences that they formerly exchanged and turning them against him now. Why does he not stop them? *Tu quoque, Brute!* If he leaped from his chair and protested, the members of the court would be grateful to him. But no, he remains seated, phlegmatic or slightly contemptuous. He is the Jew, accustomed for so many centuries not to rise in protest against outrage. However, two or three times he raised his

head, with a strange smile, as if he were saying to himself: "Insult me! Humiliate me! What does it matter?
Is not my cause that of justice and reason? Am I not
at this moment the representative of the race that had
the signal privilege of announcing the reign of justice
to the world? What contempt all these *goyim* inspire
me with!" Is not this the specific characteristic of Israel through the ages? An immense pride under the
mask of humility?

Saturday, September 2, 1899

General Deloye finished in public session his evidence
of the day before yesterday. Today his subject was not
gears, valves, and recuperators, but the specific treasonable activity attributed to Dreyfus.

The members of the court did not lose a syllable of
what he said. Moreover, the whole impression he made
was very likable. He is a fine figure of a French soldier;
short of stature, with lively features, shrewd and
sparkling eyes, swift gestures; he is a ready, lively,
and picturesque speaker, and gives one an immediate
feeling of frankness, honesty, pluck, and gameness; I
imagine that the soldiers of the Year III were like this.
He addressed the court in the most familiar tone; today
it was not their leader who was speaking, but their
comrade.

"Having had the good fortune not to have been in
any way involved in the Dreyfus case, I have an easy
conscience in giving you my opinion in all frankness.
That is why I do not hesitate to tell you that I do not

know of a single fact that establishes the prisoner's guilt. .... On the other hand, I am of the opinion that his rank and employment made it possible for him to procure the information enumerated in the *bordereau*. .... Finally, I repeat that, if I had proofs one way or the other, I should give them to you. But I have not.''

In the mouth of a general these very moderate words were of enormous importance because they amounted to ''no proof against Dreyfus.'' Maître Demange, who saw the effect this had on the minds of the members of the court, cunningly refrained from pressing him; with his usual dexterity, he took note of the statement and left it at that. But that fool Labori, imagining that Deloye could no longer escape him, started badgering and harassing him in the hope of getting some further concession. But the general suddenly burst out and said in a terrible voice:

''Don't insist! Don't insist! There are things in the *bordereau* that show that the writer was a master, and that he was at the source—at the source, you see what I mean!''

This offensive, as sudden as it was unexpected, caused a shudder to go right through the hall.

During the adjournment a few minutes later, Coupois, the clerk of the court, said to me:

''General Deloye has just pronounced the verdict of guilty.''

''The verdict has already been pronounced,'' I answered, ''but now's there's no more appeal from it.''

While we were filing back into the court through the

lawyers' robing-room, Maître Labori took me by the sleeve.

"It's going badly, isn't it?" he said.

I did not answer. He understood. Then, squeezing my arm and quivering with anger, he said:

"Listen to what I am saying. If they convict, it means revolution! We shall never disarm! And it is not they who will win! They have no real strength! With faces like that! You have seen the procession of them at the bar, the idiots, the freaks! No, no, they have no real strength. Well, if they convict, I'll give myself a month's rest, and then get back into harness. But I shall take hostages without delay!"

Indeed he did not delay, for as soon as the court resumed he took hold of General Gonse, wrapped him up in his stupidity, and shook him mercilessly.

This afternoon I could immediately detect the deep impression made on the members of the court by General Deloye's vigorous offensive. One phrase above all stuck in their minds: "The author of the *bordereau* is a master ... and was at the source. ..." They naturally applied that phrase to Dreyfus; I naturally apply it to the fourth party to the treason, the confederate of Esterhazy, Weil, Henry, the highly-placed X, who is very well known to Major Lauth and Mme Henry.

As I sat down to dinner Du Halgouët handed me a telegram from the Quai d'Orsay saying: "The Minister wishes to talk to you tomorrow morning." I shall take the train at twenty minutes after midnight.

After arriving from Rennes this morning, I went to the Quai d'Orsay at nine o'clock.

Delavaud, the Minister's deputy principal private secretary, said to me:

"The Prime Minister and the Foreign Minister are away from Paris; but you are invited to go to the Place Beauvau, where the principal private secretary to M. René Waldeck-Rousseau, the Prime Minister, has an official communication to make to you. I have not the slightest idea what it is about."

A quarter of an hour later I was at the Place Beauvau. I quote word-for-word what the Prime Minister's principal private secretary said to me:

"The Prime Minister, in agreement with M. Delcassé, has instructed me to inform you that he has information from a good source that the German Government has decided to publish the documents delivered to it in 1894 if Dreyfus is again convicted. M. Waldeck-Rousseau therefore asks you to take advantage of the confidence that has been so happily established between you and the members of the court to pass on this information to them."

"What you tell me surprises me greatly," I said. "I have difficulty in believing that Germany has decided to publish the documents delivered to her in 1894; for they would not only acquit Dreyfus and convict Esterhazy, but also reveal to us no doubt other trails that the General Staff in the Königsplatz certainly has no desire to expose."

"Nevertheless I assure you that the information that has reached the Prime Minister comes from a dependable source, and that you can safely communicate it to the members of the court. . . . Only yesterday General de Galliffet again told M. Waldeck-Rousseau that the members of the court like talking to you."

"It is true that they show a certain freedom in talking to me. I see them every afternoon in the court office, where they come to look at the documents. But I should immediately lose their confidence if I abandoned the reserve with which I have made it my duty to behave toward them. I never talk to them about the trial unless they broach the subject. . . . It is thus impossible for me to agree to the Prime Minister's proposal."

The principal private secretary continued in a disappointed tone:

"Would you have the same objection to discussing the matter with the prosecution?"

"My relations with the prosecution are freer and my scruples less. Major Carrière is the official representative of the Government; I therefore have a right to address all communications relating to the case to him; it is for him to decide whether it is his duty to submit them to the court and if so, in what form. But I shall not act in the matter except on a direct order from my official chief, M. Delcassé. . . . Meanwhile M. Waldeck-Rousseau should, in my opinion, make every effort to check the strange information that has reached him, and in particular should have it recorded in a form that will make it possible to submit it *legally* to the court. If, contrary to all the probabilities, the decision attributed to the Berlin Chancellery were put into effect, the court could rightly reproach us for having failed to warn it."

The principal private secretary promised faithfully to report our conversation to the Prime Minister.

I went back to the Quai d'Orsay and quickly wrote a memorandum for Delcassé, who is returning to Paris this evening.

At midday I left for Rennes again.

Monday, September 4, 1899

Colonel Jouaust, using his discretionary powers, called on an unexpected witness, who came forward spontaneously with an offer of "grave revelations." He is Eugen Lazar von Czernusky, a former lieutenant of Austrian dragoons, aged thirty-one.

As he speaks French only with difficulty, his written statement of evidence was read by the clerk of the court. He said that one of his friends, "the head of a department at the Ministry of Foreign Affairs in Vienna," had told him in confidence in August, 1894, "the names of four persons who were engaged in espionage in France on behalf of the Germanic powers"; the first of these four names was that of Captain Dreyfus. A month later, *i.e.*, in September, Czernusky had met at Geneva a high officer of the German General Staff who had fully confirmed the assertions of his friend, the Vienna diplomatist. Czernusky added that since 1896 he had been in contact with the French intelligence service.

During the reading of this evidence I looked closely at this strange witness. His appearance should have been enough to discredit him. His complexion was haggard, there was a shifty look in his rheumy, twitching eyes, his ears were asymmetrical, and he was continually grimacing. His face was that of a rogue and vagabond; the man was obviously a social outcast.

The members of the court were obviously taken completely aback by the appearance of this witness and seemed to be wondering what this unexpected turn of events could possibly mean.

Major Carrière, using very cautious language, as if he felt he were on dangerous ground, asked that the sitting should be continued *in camera.*

But Labori in his wrath rose to his full height, and thundered:

"In the first place I make the most complete reservations about the evidence of this Herr von Czernusky. And since the other side has suddenly introduced into this trial the evidence of a foreigner, I wish to announce that I shall make an application to the court with a view to a request being made through diplomatic channels for the documents enumerated in the *bordereau,* so that they may be laid before the court."

Czernusky was thereupon invited to come back to-morrow morning to complete his evidence *in camera,* and the court adjourned.

After a few minutes' discussion among themselves, the members of the court sent for me and asked me my opinion about Maître Labori's proposed application. I had no hesitation in replying that M. Delcassé would certainly not agree to the request's being forwarded to Berlin.

When the court resumed the proceedings dragged on for another four hours; they were concerned with police tittle-tattle and police dodges, all entirely devoid of interest.

This afternoon the members of the court had a long conference in their room. When they came out none of them spoke to me. I was struck by the gravity of their expression.

On the stroke of six Major Carrière came into my office; I was no less struck by his worried look.

"The situation is becoming serious," he said. "The court is in an *impasse,* from which the Government must help to extricate it. So tomorrow I shall associate myself with Maître Labori's plea and ask the court to accept it. I thought I ought to warn you."

"If you make such a request to the court, I shall protest," I replied. "M. Delcassé would certainly never stoop to soliciting German aid in solving a judicial problem coming exclusively under French jurisdiction."

I also reminded the major of the semi-official statement in the *Cologne Gazette* of August 16 which peremptorily rejected the possibility that the documents handed over in 1894 might be made available, as the Imperial Chancellery had no wish to expose itself to their being declared false.

The worthy major several times shook his old bird's head and looked tragically comic.

"What a fix we're in!" he exclaimed. "What a fix! . . . So you see no way of helping us?"

It was now my turn to feel extremely embarrassed; for I no longer felt I had the right to conceal from the Government prosecutor the confidential information that I was given yesterday in the Place Beauvau. I therefore told him in confidence about the mysterious information that had reached the Prime Minister; and I did not fail to make it clear that I did not guarantee its accuracy.

"But what are you telling me?" he exclaimed, beating the air with his arms as if he were about to take wing. "Publish the documents after the conviction! But that would be terrible!"

When he had somewhat recovered from his stupefaction, he begged me to come with him to see Colonel Jouaust, whom he wished to inform of our conversation immediately. I agreed to do so, on condition that I should wait outside the colonel's house until I received a direct invitation to enter.

We went there with all speed. The colonel is staying on the other bank of the Vilaine, in the peaceful quarter which surrounds the cathedral. On the way I said to Carrière:

"You were telling me the other day that you had no doubt that Dreyfus was guilty. In that case, why do you think it would be dreadful if Germany published the 1894 documents in the event of another conviction?"

His long experience of military justice inspired this profoundly philosophical reply:

"It's never a good thing for secret documents to be published. The public always wants more. One thing leads to another, and you can never tell what it will lead to."

Meanwhile we had reached the house where Colonel Jouaust was staying. The prosecuting officer went in alone.

Five minutes later the presiding officer came and fetched me. The modest, old-fashioned little drawing-room into which he led me made an attractive background to Colonel Jouaust's honest appearance.

Our deliberations did not last long. When I explained to the colonel that we could not decently ask the Germans to oblige us by extricating us from a difficulty, and that in any case a request to them to do so would in all probability meet with a refusal, the colonel promptly agreed with me. Finally he said to me:

"I shall confidentially pass on to my colleagues the information given to you in Paris yesterday, and I shall add that you cannot guarantee its correctness; they will form their own estimate of its value. But, as it is important that everyone should accept his own responsibilities, I shall call you to the bar tomorrow morning as soon as the court opens so that you may publicly state the attitude of the Foreign Ministry to Maître Labori's application."

While accompanying me to the front door Jouaust said to me:

"What was your impression of Czernusky?"

"That of a scoundrel and a false witness."

Neither the presiding nor the prosecuting officer contradicted me.

Tuesday, September 5, 1899

The court sat *in camera* and Czernusky finished his evidence.

The police information that has been obtained about him is very damaging. The son of an epileptic and a lunatic, suffering from mental troubles himself, a deserter from the Austrian army, riddled with debts, he lives by crime and from hand to mouth. Mystery surrounds his relations with the intelligence service.

Thus nothing was left of the fine assurance that he affected yesterday. Harassed with questions by the two lawyers, he collapsed pitifully. He also complained of a violent migraine. The members of the court listened to him with visible uneasiness, for, as I have just been informed, they knew that since his arrival at Rennes he had had conferences with General Mercier and General Roget.

During the adjournment Captain Beauvais said to me:

"That was a customer who should not have been shown us!"

As soon as the proceeding *in camera* had been concluded and the court was opened to the public again, Maître Labori submitted his plea "that the French Government should be asked to intervene through diplomatic channels with the interested powers with a view to the submission to the court-martial of the documents enumerated in the *bordereau."* He spoke in a combative tone, and with ample gestures.

While he was concluding his arguments, Du Halgouët handed me an urgent telegram that he had just decoded. It was Delcassé's answer to the information I gave him yesterday and was as follows: "I have no knowledge whatever whether the documents enumerated in the *bordereau* are in the possession of Germany; consequently I do not know whether she proposes to publish them in the event of Dreyfus' being again convicted." ... Now, only the day before yesterday, they summoned me to Paris for the purpose of officially telling me the very opposite and instructing me to inform the members of the court accordingly!

But there was no time to reflect on the matter, for Colonel Jouaust summoned me to the bar and asked me as the representative of the Ministry of Foreign Affairs to state the Ministry's attitude to Maître Labori's application.

I said:

"Gentlemen, I understand very well the importance that Captain Dreyfus' counsel attach to having the documents enumerated in the *bordereau* produced in court, for they constitute the very crux of the case. Though the application made on the prisoner's behalf seems based on logic and on justice, from the diplomatic point of view it is unacceptable. Considerations of the highest order prevent the Government of the Republic from taking the initiative in relation to a foreign power that is asked of it. If the court requires further clarification of the matter, I request that I may be asked for it *in camera*."

The court accepted my statement and unanimously rejected Maître Labori's application.

Maître Labori then announced that in the incontestable exercise of his rights, he summoned Colonel Schwartzkoppen and Colonel Panizzardi to appear before the court as witnesses.

The whole hall rose at these words, in either protest or applause.

When silence had been re-established a solemn and austere person approached the bar, one of the first converts to the Dreyfusist faith and one of its protomartyrs, Senator Trarieux, the former Keeper of the Seals. However worthy of respect, even moving, he may be in the ingenuousness of his apostolic fervor, the members of the court surreptitiously cast angry looks at him, for he had obtained all his arguments, which he presented with admirable logic, from the German and Italian Ambassadors. While he was delivering his peroration, without for one moment suspecting the disastrous effect that he was producing, I recalled ironically that according to the ancient Jewish law the punishment for any prophecy made in the name of strange gods, *even if it were true*, was to be burned alive.

After the sitting was over, I sent a telegram to Delcassé saying that the state of feeling among the public, and particularly among the military, was such that I regarded with grave apprehension the possibility that Colonel Schwartzkoppen and Colonel Panizzardi might come to Rennes to give evidence; their appearance here might lead to shocking scenes, both in court and in the streets.

At about six o'clock the prefect and the director of the Sûreté Générale came to see me in my office.

"You cannot conceive the anger that this morning's sitting has provoked throughout the town," the prefect said to me. "The bourgeois and business section of the population is still restraining itself, but the workers in the outskirts are in a state of tumult. As for the garrison—officers and troops alike—they talk of nothing but throwing the Dreyfusards into the Vilaine. You can be certain that, if Schwartzkoppen and Panizzardi appeared in court, there would be violence. They would be hissed and cursed and, I fear, perhaps worse than that. Don't forget the attempt to murder Labori!"

My only answer was to show my visitors the telegram that I had already sent to Delcassé.

Wednesday, September 6, 1899

The guileless and pontificating Trarieux complacently finished his disastrous evidence.

After this Maître Labori, more in form than ever, took some generals and harried them, hustled them, and reduced them to pulp. He handled them so roughly that Colonel Jouaust ended by calling him to order.

"Maître Labori," he said, "I invite you to express yourself with moderation."

"I have not said a single word that was not moderate."

"But your tone is not."

"I am not the master of my tone."

"Very well, master it, then! Otherwise I shall ask you to stop speaking."

"Stop me, then."

"I withdraw your right to speak."

"I bow to that. But I ask it to be noted that I am silenced as soon as I advance into territory on which I cannot be resisted."

"Sit down!"

"I sit down, sir, but not at your orders, but because I choose to sit down."

Maître Demange and Dreyfus listened to this exchange with terror on their faces.

On the way out after the end of the sitting, while we were still in the little school courtyard, I was button-holed by several members of the court—Brongniart, Profillet, Bréon, Parfait, and Beauvais. Brongniart said:

"Do you believe the Government will authorize the appearance in court of Schwartzkoppen and Panizzardi?"

"I have received no instructions on that subject. But, between ourselves, I cannot see M. Delcassé arranging for foreign military attachés to discuss their espionage operations before a French court-martial."

Brongniart answered coldly:

"Bravo for M. Delcassé!"

At eight o'clock this evening, while I was at dinner, I was handed the Minister's answer to my telegrams and telephone messages of the day. It was as follows:

"Please inform prosecution and defense that only possible way of procuring evidence of Colonels Schwartzkoppen and Panizzardi is by sending a rogatory commission."

I went immediately to the Hôtel de France, where
Maître Demange is staying.

All the chiefs, champions, missionaries, and prose-
lytes of Dreyfusism were gathered in the big hotel
courtyard. In spite of the stifling heat of the evening,
they were passionately holding forth and gesticulating.

As soon as I was noticed advancing into this cara-
vansary, which I had taken care not to penetrate
hitherto, the talk stopped so abruptly that mouths remained open and gestures were frozen in mid-air. I
signed to Maître Demange. He hurried toward me and
took me to his room.

Our conversation lasted for more than an hour, for
there was a conflict of grave principles. I cannot praise
highly enough the spirit in which Maître Demange conducted the discussion—a spirit of subtlety, prudence,
and high reason. He agreed to everything I asked of
him—except to discuss the question with his irascible
colleague.

"I have long since given up discussing anything
whatever with Labori," he said. "It immediately turns
to fisticuffs. Outside the court we do not speak. I must
even ask you not to mention to him that I agreed to
have this talk with you this evening."

"But you are the leading counsel for the defense," I
objected. "It is therefore natural that I should approach you first."

"Leading counsel!" he exclaimed. "That is an expression for which Labori would never forgive me if he heard you saying it. *Leading* counsel! He'd tear my eyes out for that alone! For the rest, I agree in advance to anything you get from him."

It was too late by now for me to go and see Labori, who is staying at the other end of the town. I shall see him tomorrow morning before the court sits.

Thursday, September 7, 1899

At six o'clock this morning I was at grips with Labori, trying to get him to give up insisting on the personal appearance of Schwartzkoppen and Panizzardi.

"Send them a rogatory commission," I said. "They will reply before a judge in their own country. It is the normal procedure."

Labori, bursting with indignation, replied that the rogatory commission procedure would take at least a week, while the military code of justice did not permit the adjournment of a court-martial for such a length of time; and besides, the court was obviously tired of the trial. On the other hand, if Schwartzkoppen and Panizzardi agreed, they could be at Rennes in forty-eight hours.

But I held firm.

"The Government of the Republic," I said, "is unwilling to incur responsibility for the shocking scenes that the appearance at Rennes of foreign military attachés would inevitably provoke. You will have to accept that fact."

In the end, mumbling terrible threats, he gave in.

As soon as the proceedings began, he submitted a plea that the evidence of Colonel Schwartzkoppen and Colonel Panizzardi should be taken by a rogatory commission. He added in a voice quivering with irony:

"I have in fact been unofficially warned that the personal appearance of these two most important witnesses would not be authorized."

Colonel Jouaust summoned me to the bar to make a statement. I said:

"Considerations of public order make it undesirable that foreign military attachés should appear before a French court to give evidence on matters that may have come to their knowledge in the course of their diplomatic duties. Colonels Schwartzkoppen and Panizzardi will not appear before the Rennes court-martial. As for the sending of a rogatory commission, I assume that the Minister of Foreign Affairs would have no objection."

The court decided to set aside Maître Labori's plea, so a rogatory commission will not be sent.

After a final moving intervention by General Mercier, Colonel Jouaust announced that the hearing of evidence was now concluded, whereupon the military witnesses, more than a hundred officers, rose and left the hall, in conformity with an order of the Minister of War. General de Galliffet's object in giving them this order was to restore the serenity of atmosphere of the court for the final act of the drama. No doubt he also thought that the disappearance of the accusers would somewhat liberate the minds of the members of the court. I am afraid that this calculation was vitiated by the theatrical manner in which the officers carried out their withdrawal. They did it with machine-like precision, with measured step and holding their heads erect, as if they were on maneuvers. I almost thought I heard the word of command: "By the left, right wheel, quick march!" Their whole attitude seemed to say: Our task is done; we have won the army case; the verdict is now no more than a simple formality.

Major Carrière then made the final speech for the prosecution.

The performance put up by the poor man, with his receding forehead, his small, staring eyes, his voice that was in turn yapping and sepulchral, was indescribable. The twaddle that he inflicted on us for an hour-and-a-half was so absurd, so flabby, so disjointed, so flat and incoherent, that at least twenty times the shorthand writers, having hopelessly lost the thread, put down their pens in despair. When I tried from time to time to forget the tragedy of the situation, I thought I was looking at Polichinelle or Gribouille, Jocrisse or Turlupin. The members of the court looked humiliated.

At least the old fool did not put himself out to make an eloquent peroration.

"Members of the court," he said, "I tell you that Dreyfus is guilty. I therefore demand the application of Article 76 of the penal code."

During lunch General Chamoin, looking radiant, said to me:

"After a final speech for the prosecution of such complete nullity, Dreyfus' acquittal is certain. I have just telephoned General de Galliffet to say so."

"And I have just telephoned M. Delcassé saying that a conviction is inevitable."

Friday, September 8, 1899

It was Maître Demange's turn to speak; his speech took five hours and was interrupted only for a few minutes' rest. It was a fine speech, with no care for eloquence or ornament, but solid, clear, sensible, moderate, courteous, infused throughout with frankness, good sense, and pity. The members of the court seemed moved by it. Does that make an acquittal possible, or probable? No. *Alea jacta est.*

At half-past nine, during the adjournment, Lieutenant-Colonel Brongniart came over to me.

"Have you heard anything from Paris since yesterday?"

"What about?"

"About the documents delivered in 1894."

"No, I have received no new information."

He remained thoughtful. But Captain Beauvais touched him on the shoulder.

"The court is about to resume, sir!"

"All right, go along. I'll rejoin you in the vestibule. I am just finishing asking M. Paléologue something."

We remained alone in the yard. Then, looking into my eyes, Brongniart gravely asked me:

"Do you solemnly and sincerely believe that the documents enumerated in the *bordereau* are in Berlin?"

"I believe so, but I have no proof."

"Do you solemnly and sincerely believe that Ger-

many has decided to publish these documents if Dreyfus is convicted again?''

''I have no reason to believe so. But, if such publication took place, I am sure that it would exonerate Dreyfus completely.''

''Thank you.''

We quickly rejoined the other members of the court,
who were waiting for us before entering the courtroom.

Last night the Lord Chief Justice of England, Lord
Russell of Killowen, arrived at Rennes. I was given
orders to put myself at his disposal and to procure him
a seat on the platform, next to me.

At half-past five this morning I offered him a substantial ''breakfast'' [11] washed down with a bottle of
dry Chablis. After giving him a substantial meal, I
took him along to the court.

After the first words that we exchanged, Lord Russell strongly criticized the conduct of the trial.

''I shall not conceal from you that I am shocked,''
he said. ''What an offense against justice is this interminable procession of accusers before the bar! A
witness has no right to accuse; he must say what he
saw, what he knows, and no more. Why this complais-
ance toward the prosecution? Why did the presiding
officer permit it? And this prosecutor, whose final
speech I read yesterday, what feebleness, what ignorance of the law! How could such a grave task be entrusted to 'such a grotesque figure?' [12] Does France

[11] This word in English in the original.
[12] These words in English in the original.

not know that the eyes of the world are on the Dreyfus case?''

To these criticisms, which were stated with an entirely British arrogance and abruptness, I replied:

''Painful though it is to me to hear what you say, I am glad that you have come to Rennes; for you will see how thoroughly and conscientiously the members of the court-martial will carry out their duty. I have been living in close contact with them daily for thirty-three days. I assure you that they deserve all your esteem and all your respect. If there are among them some who do not yet see the truth, it is not their fault.''

Lord Russell took his place on the platform between General Chamoin and myself.

When the *gendarmes* brought in the prisoner, the Lord Chief Justice looked at him with fascination, half raising himself in his chair to see him better. Then, sitting back suddenly, he whispered into my ear in astonishment:

''What an unattractive-looking man!''

He listened carefully to Maître Demange's speech, of which he did not lose a syllable.

At midday, when I took him back to the hotel for lunch, he was much less severe in his strictures than he had been in the morning.

''I liked Maître Demange's speech very much,'' he said. ''I thought it clear, sensible, well constructed. . . . All the same, with us counsel would not have permitted himself any appeal to the emotions. When you are in the right, you must remain cold.''

At seven o'clock I took him to dine at a country inn,

under some high trees beneath which there had once strayed the enchanter Merlin and the fairy Viviane.

Throughout the meal Lord Russell, in whom there was no more trace of his morning spleen, explained the philosophy of the Dreyfus case to me from an English lawyer's point of view; and I could thus judge the extent to which the French mind, which is so open to the sense of justice, is closed to the notion of law.

Saturday, September 9, 1899

Maître Demange finished his speech with a peroration which was very short, very sober, but very powerful by reason of the warmth with which it was spoken and the elevation of his thought; he visibly touched the hearts of the members of the court.

"Yes," he said, "the prisoner before you, this martyr, I proclaim him innocent. I declare that your verdict will not be a verdict of guilty because you are not only honest, but also enlightened men. Now, the members of the 1894 court were not enlightened; they had not seen Esterhazy's handwriting; you have seen it. That is the leading thread; God has granted that it be put into your hands. Now, members of the court, go! I have finished my task. Do yours! I pray God that He may enlighten your consciences and restore to our country the harmony of which it has so much need."

The moral resonance of this peroration was, as it were, sustained and prolonged by the fact that Maître Labori, who was calm and dignified for the first time, simply said:

"I renounce my right to speak."

As it was already midday and the prosecutor intended to reply, the court adjourned; it is to resume at three o'clock.

In our cloakroom, where the members of the court waited for a moment to avoid the public streaming out of the school, I could not help feeling sharp emotion at the sight of the anxious expressions, the dark eyes, the pallid or blue faces of Jouaust, Brongniart, Profillet, Bréon, Beauvais, Parfait, and even the imperturbable Merle.

"Look at them!" Chamoin said to me. "Look at them! If that's how they look, they won't convict."

"May God grant that you are right!"

When I got back to the hotel for lunch, I was handed a telegram from the Quai d'Orsay. It was as follows:

REPRESENTATIVE FOREIGN MINISTRY—RENNES.
EXTREMELY URGENT.

Here is an extract from official part of yesterday's Reichsanzeiger: *"We are authorized to repeat the statements that the Imperial Government has made several times already on the subject of Captain Dreyfus. We declare once more and in the most formal fashion that there have never been any dealings whatever, whether direct or indirect, between this officer and any German agent."*

What was I to do with this information? The Minister had refrained from giving me any instructions.

After long reflection, I decided to refrain from any

approach whatever to the court. I decided that the
hearing of evidence having concluded two days ago,
my re-entry on the stage would look like a maneuver
in extremis and, above all, that if there were any statement whatever that could yet save Dreyfus, it would
not be a statement coming from abroad.

At half-past two I made my way back to the court.

The town was seething with excitement and there
was an enormous crowd round the school. The whole
garrison had been turned out; patrols of gunners,
dragoons, and *gendarmes* were everywhere.

Outside I met the director of the Sûreté Générale,
who said to me:

"You are going to hear a very strong reply by Major
Carrière. Don't be surprised; it's not his own; it has
just been sent him by a great friend of General Mercier's, the Nationalist lawyer Jules Auffray."

"How do you know?"

"From the person whom they had the imprudence
to ask to deliver it."

The court resumed at three o'clock precisely, and
Major Carrière spoke.

His reply, of which he was obviously not the author,
summed up in a few phrases of striking brevity the
duties that devolve upon members of a court-martial
when the time has come for them to consider their
verdict.

"You have heard much evidence," he said. "I call
on you to divide it in your minds into two parts: that
which points to the prisoner's innocence, and that
which points to his guilt. . . . In a case like this proof

does not reside in this point or in that; it is everywhere; it emerges from the case as a whole. . . . You are not only the judges, but also the jury. Now, the law does not call on members of a jury to render an account of the reasons by which they arrive at their verdict; it calls on them only to declare what they believe in their hearts. . . . That, members of the court, is the spirit of the law. I say no more. The time for speeches has passed. For you the hour of supreme decision has struck. France anxiously awaits your verdict. As for myself, still firm in my original belief, I call on you to apply Article 76 of the penal code."

Maître Demange, who seemed at the end of his strength, said in a stifled voice:

"And this is my last word, gentlemen. Men of your rectitude will never elevate to the level of a proof the vague possibilities that have been presented to you here."

Finally, Colonel Jouaust said to the accused:

"Captain Dreyfus, have you anything to add to your defense?"

Dreyfus, who looked like a corpse, muttered some indistinct words:

"I am innocent. . . . The honor of the name my children bear. . . . Your honesty, your justice. . . ."

And he fell back on his chair. Sweat was pouring from his brow.

At three-fifteen, the members of the court rose and retired to their room.

General Chamoin, Major Carrière, and I went out

into the little yard where all the "entr'actes" had been passed.

We had to wait for an hour-and-a-half. We walked up and down, smoking cigarettes, guessing only too well why the deliberations were lasting so long.

I could have killed Major Carrière, so intolerable was the old clown's chatter. Seeing how worried the general and I were, he tried to distract us by the most inept jokes, each more preposterous than the last.

At four-forty-five a bell rang.

In a second the hall was full. But the setting was somewhat changed. A line of *gendarmes* was standing in front of the platform, facing the public for violent demonstrations against the members of the court were feared. A squad of infantry had also been posted at each door. For the moment, however, there was not a sound. So deep was the silence that it seemed as if the whole hall were holding its breath.

Maître Labori was seated stiffly and stoically on the counsels' bench with arms crossed and a bellicose look in his eyes; Maître Demange sat bent, with his eyes closed, and his hands joined in prayer.

The prisoner's chair was vacant because, in accordance with the military code, he must not be present at the pronouncement of the verdict.

At last the judges came in, all horribly pale.

Colonel Jouaust read the judgment of the court in a voice which choked over the first words:

"In the name of the French people! The court-martial, by a majority of five votes to two, declares: Yes, the prisoner is guilty. There are attenuating circumstances . . . in consequence of which the court sentences Alfred Dreyfus to ten years' detention."

The public, so far from demonstrating, seemed struck dumb; it flowed out into the street, without a murmur.

When the hall was empty, I said good-by to the members of the court, whose faces were still overwrought.

Then I went back to the office to pack my files. Soon afterward I saw the clerk of the court, Coupois, who had just read the judgment of the court to Dreyfus. During this formality, which was carried out before an armed guard, the prisoner stood rigid, without betraying the slightest emotion.

I left Rennes, with General Chamoin, by the nine o'clock train. The crowd that had invaded the station was in such a paroxysm of rage or passion that we were smuggled into the station by a side door.

In the compartment that had been reserved for us, we talked until after midnight. Comparing our memories and impressions, we thought we were able to decide that the two members of the Court who had voted for acquittal were Colonel Jouaust and Major de Bréon, the first because he had found illumination in his free-thinker's conscience, the second in his Catholic conscience. But what had happened in the conscience of the five others?

Sunday, September 10, 1899

At nine o'clock this morning I was received by Delcassé, to whom I went to render an account of my mission.

As soon as he saw me he exclaimed:
"Wretch! What have you done? . . . You gave the
court the extract from the *Reichsanzeiger*!"

"No, Mr. Minister, I did not, even unofficially. . . ."

I was preparing to give him my reasons, but he was
no longer listening. With his face wreathed in smiles,
he exclaimed:

"My dear fellow, my dear, dear fellow, I was sure
of you! You realized perfectly that I sent you that for
yourself alone, for your own personal information. . . .
You know that I have always been unwilling to seek
German help. All the same, read what they have dared
to say about me!"

He passed me the *Écho de Paris*, which had the following in bold type:

France must be told that she has a Foreign Minister
who has not shrunk from compounding with a foreign
country. The German official statement published in the
Reichsanzeiger *was asked for by M. Delcassé, who had*
it submitted to the court-martial by M. Paléologue.

While I read this piece, Delcassé started feverishly
writing out a stinging rejoinder which he at once sent
to the Havas agency.

When I had finished describing the final stages of
the trial to him, I said:

"May I be told how the Prime Minister came to believe that if Dreyfus were again convicted, Germany
would publish the documents delivered in 1894? Where
did his information come from? And why did he in-

struct me to pass it on to the members of the court, since two days later you telegraphed me that you could not in any way guarantee it?''

Delcassé, showing signs of great vexation, told me with much circumlocution that Waldeck-Rousseau had on his own account, over the head of his Foreign Minister, applied to Berlin to have the documents enumerated in the *bordereau* handed to the French Government for submission to the court-martial. As was to be expected, the negotiations had been completely unsuccessful. That was the background to the dishonest intrigue in which an attempt had been made to involve me. The Minister ended with these words:

''Forget all that! Forget it!''

He kept me for nearly an hour longer. He said no more about the Dreyfus case but talked about his political program. With sparkling eyes he said to me:

''War will soon break out in the Transvaal.[13] It will be a terrible blow for England. She will need us. She will have to choose between Germany and us, and at all costs she must choose us. It's a magnificent game to play! We have a trump card to play: Russia ....

....

....

Decidedly there is a touch of Mazarin about this man.

Friday, September 15, 1899

I received the following letter from the Minister.

[13] The Boer War in fact broke out on October 13th.

Sir,

I am happy to be able to assure you of my complete satisfaction with the manner in which, as the representative of the Ministry of Foreign Affairs, you carried out the task entrusted to you in connection with the court-martial at Rennes and the Dreyfus case.

You succeeded, in conformity with my instructions, in bringing to that task the reserve and the tact required by the delicate nature of the case, and it was with pleasure that I observed that you never failed to answer the questions put to you with perfect clarity and dignity.

I have appreciated in altogether special fashion the attitude that you preserved throughout the course of the trial, and I desire to convey to you, together with my personal thanks, this expression of my most lively congratulations.

Yours, etc.,

(signed)   Delcassé

EPILOGUE

On September 19, 1899, General de Galliffet, the Minister of War, submitted for the signature of the President of the Republic a decree granting Dreyfus a remission of his sentence.

In justification of this act of grace, General de Galliffet pleaded "the gravely compromised health of the convicted man." He added: "After a difficult crisis, a higher political interest, the necessity of rallying all their strength, has always imposed on governments measures of clemency, pacification, and forgetfulness."

Waldeck-Rousseau, taking inspiration from the same thought, soon afterward caused the two Chambers to pass a full and complete amnesty for all crimes and misdemeanors that might have been committed in connection with the Dreyfus case.

Henceforward, for lack of nourishment, passions

gradually subsided; hatred and rancor lost their edge; time did its work. Death helped greatly by removing some of the most ardent among the leading spirits, such as, Scheurer-Kestner, Cavaignac, Trarieux, Zola, etc. Soon honorable words were actually exchanged between the two camps. Thus in the spring of 1903, when the great scholar Gaston Pâris died, one of his friends, from whom he became estranged during the crisis, Eugène-Melchior de Vogüé, paid him this public tribute: "Where except at the edge of this tomb would one say what must be cried aloud for the honor of our country? Above squalid interest and animal passions, the bravest hearts of France rushed against each other in the night with equal disinterestedness, with equal nobility."

Meanwhile several apocryphal or concealed documents were discovered at the War Ministry that threw unexpected light on the Dreyfus case.

On March 3, 1904, the Cour de Cassation took up the case again. All the surviving witnesses, General Mercier, General de Boisdeffre, General Gonse, General Roget, Colonel du Paty de Clam, Major Lauth, Picquart, the archivist Gribelin, ex-President Casimir-Perier, Hanotaux, etc., etc., appeared all over again. I myself had to go to court and hark back over the old story.

But this old melodrama now seemed so out-of-date, people were so heartily sick of it, that nobody took any interest except a few professional slanderers, who might have been beating the air for all the impression they made.

At last, after very long and very prudent delays and in a completely pacified atmosphere, on June 12, 1906, the Supreme Court, at a combined session of all its Chambers, delivered a judgment that ended as follows:

For these reasons
the Court
Annuls the verdict of the Rennes court-martial that sentenced Dreyfus to ten years' detention,
Declares that he was convicted wrongly and in error.

The detailed "considerations" that led the court to this decision fill no fewer than forty pages, and are an irrefutable demonstration of Dreyfus' innocence.[1]

But the puzzle of the identity of the guilty men of 1894 remains unsolved and will remain unsolved until the Berlin archives yield up their secret.

[1] On the day after his vindication in court, a law passed by 432 votes to 32 in the Chamber of Deputies and by 182 votes to 30 in the Senate reinstated him in the army with the rank of major. He was appointed a Chevalier of the Legion of Honor on July 20 and posted to the fort of Vincennes, where he resumed duty on October 15, twelve years to the day after his arrest. He was put on the retired list on June 26, 1907, but returned to active service on August 2, 1914. He was first assigned to the staff of the artillery of the entrenched camp of Paris, and then, in 1917, to a divisional artillery park of the 20th Army Corps; and finally, at the beginning of 1918, he was appointed to the artillery park of the 5th Region and promoted to lieutenant-colonel of the reserve. Colonel Dreyfus died of a heart affection on July 11, 1935.

INDEX

311

Date Due

Date Due			
OCT 15 '68			
NOV 20 1967			
FEB 1 1969			
MAY 7 1970			
MAR 26 1972			
NOV 5 1972			
OCT 21 1974			
SEP 22 1975			
NOV 14 1975			
NOV 7 1977			
FEB 17 1980			
FE23 81			
ℊℬ	PRINTED	IN U. S. A.	